Where's GOD? on Monday

Alistair MACKENZIE
Wayne KIRKLAND

HENDRICKSON
PUBLISHERS

THEOLOGY OF WORK   PROJECT

Where's God on Monday?

© 2015 Hendrickson Publishers Marketing, LLC
P. O. Box 3473
Peabody, Massachusetts 01961-3473
www.hendrickson.com

ISBN 978-1-61970-707-8

Printed in the United States of America

First Printing—December 2015

Library of Congress Cataloging-in-Publication Data

Mackenzie, Alistair, 1947–
     Where's God on Monday? / Alistair Mackenzie and
Wayne Kirkland.
          pages cm
     Originally published: Colorado Springs, CO : NavPress, c2003.
     Includes bibliographical references.
     ISBN 978-1-61970-707-8 (alk. paper)
     1. Work—Religious aspects—Christianity. 2. Christian life.
I. Kirkland, Wayne. II. Title.
     BT738.5.M28 2015
     248.8'8   dc23
                    2015030624

Contents

INTRODUCTION

Where's God On Monday?

ROGER

Roger is a workaholic. He wouldn't admit it, but his life certainly bears the fruit of it. Roger is also a Christian and feels a deep sense of call to his profession in law. The work of a demanding practice means that 70-to-80-hour weeks are the norm for Roger. But he also contributes in the church that he and his family are part of. He's on several committees, leads worship and a home group, and is prominent in many other ways.

People who know Roger certainly esteem him highly. He's incredibly busy doing important work, making a major contribution to God's kingdom. At least that's what both Roger and his friends believe.

But there's another side to him, which is not so obvious. Roger finds it difficult to say no. He's desperate for people's approval and affirmation and, as a result, is close to burnout. So is his family. His wife Colleen is resigned to things always being this way, even in "retirement." She copes as best she can and carries the extra load in parenting and household tasks. Secretly, she dreams of getting off the treadmill they're on, but deep down she knows Roger would either quickly die—or find another equally demanding treadmill to leap onto!

KAREN

Karen is married to Steve and is mother to three growing boys. Before having children, she was a secretary in a busy office. Highly skilled, she used to find conversation easy at dinner parties and when meeting new people.

But now, several years on, she doesn't know what to say when people ask, "Do you work?" Though she uses the positive reply, "I'm a full-time mother," she detects a certain lack of interest— sometimes almost disparagement. Not only does Karen believe she is undervalued by her peers for a task she feels passionately about, but there is also no easy way to describe the myriad of other ways she contributes during the week—such as voluntary work at school, in the community, and through friendships.

On top of all of this, Karen feels no small amount of peer pressure to "get a job," like all of her friends who are now "going back to work." She and Steve, however, both feel that the time is not right, and that the benefits of having one of them at home for the children are worth the cost.

JOSEPH

Joseph works in a bank, but he's not intending to stick around too long. He's frustrated by the limitations put on his witness and has plans to get into "full-time Christian service." He feels called to pastoring and regards the job at the bank as a way to earn the dollars needed to go to Bible college.

Joseph has been particularly inspired by a couple of visiting preachers who have encouraged him to "aim high" and not settle for second best. He feels that he could be so much more effective for the Lord by giving all his time and energy to pastoring. The elders in his church have been supportive of this aim, giving him opportunity to try his hand at preaching and involving him in other areas of leadership within the church.

MARK

Mark faces a dilemma. He's a middle manager, and the demands his employer places on him get bigger every year. More responsibility, harder deadlines, better results—these are what the bosses seem to be after. Trying to add family commitments (he has a wife and two young children) and church involvement is creating an unbearable burden. Already he leaves home at 6:45 a.m. to beat the rush-hour traffic, and gets home around 7:00 p.m., just in time to put the kids to bed. He regularly takes work home nights and weekends.

Mark is caught in a bind. He knows that if he slackens off on his "work," then his job will be at risk. But the worst thing is that his job is so all-consuming. Outside of "work hours" he finds it difficult to give people his full attention. He just doesn't have the energy for proper preparation of his home-group sessions or for spending time with his kids and wife—much less getting involved in a club or community activity.

He feels guilty about all this but doesn't know what to do. Church doesn't help—particularly Sunday services, which seem totally unrelated to his "real life," almost as if they're in a different world.

JULIE

Julie is unemployed. At least that's how the Department of Statistics lists her. But it hasn't always been this way. Five years ago she was made redundant (fired) and hasn't been able to find a job since. Julie suspects it's because of her age. No one really wants to employ a 58-year-old. In spite of her best attempts to keep positive, five years of job interviews, rejection letters, and telling people she's "between jobs" have worn her down. Julie is now hanging out for retirement.

Sadly, her confidence and self-esteem are so undermined that she doesn't see how much potential there is for her to contribute on a voluntary basis. Although a church or community organization would be eager to snap up her skills, she is careful not to get actively involved in the ones she has links with. Julie regards them more as a "fill-in"—second best to a "real job."

THE SUNDAY-MONDAY SPLIT

Five people—all Christians, struggling with what it means to work and follow Jesus (although these stories are based on real people, we have altered names and some of the details). The issues are many and complex. This book seeks to give some perspectives to the Karens and Marks and Rogers—and many others who genuinely want to be faithful to Jesus in all they do, yet struggle to know how to do this in their daily work. They are representative of hundreds of Christians we have spoken with over the years. In fact, the epilogue to this book shares how many of these conversations have contributed to our writing.

The sad truth is that much of our church life completely ignores the subject of daily work, as if what people do for most of their week has little connection with their faith. As Calvin Redekop (a Canadian Mennonite) has noted, the truth is that average Christians spend less than 2 percent of their waking time at church and most of their time working. Yet the church puts most of its energy and resources into that 2 percent and very little into the world of daily work.

Work is the dominant activity of our everyday lives, and yet so often our work and worship end up having little to do with each other. An enormous chasm lies between the worlds of Sunday and Monday. That's the problem. What about some solutions?

Where's God on Monday? is a starting point. It grapples with some of the issues from a biblical perspective. We're not aiming for some pie-in-the-sky theologizing, but rather, intensely practical and tangible outworkings for our day-to-day work. To help you contextualize matters within your own work life, we've developed some exercises and questions at the end of each chapter. They are useful for both individual and group reflection. Before we go any further, however, there's a fundamental issue we need to address: How we understand and use the word *work*.

WHO IS WORKING?

Imagine this scene: It's 6:00 p.m. and John walks in through the front entrance of the house he shares with Liz, his wife, and their three children. He puts down his briefcase and Liz immediately gives him a kiss, inquiring, "How was your *day at work*, dear?"

John automatically knows what his wife is asking. He's employed as an accountant for forty hours a week at a firm downtown. Liz is asking him how his *paid job* went today. After a short commentary on the office politics and a struggle sorting out a client's books, John returns the favor by asking Liz, "So how was your *day at home*?"

John never thinks to ask, "How was your *day of work at home*?" Liz knows she has also been working today. And we hope John doesn't think she has just been lazing around or resting while he's been gone! Taking care of three young active boys, looking after the house, preparing the meals, and volunteering at the boys' school have all filled Liz's day. She has been working hard, but the words John uses don't overtly acknowledge this.

Unfortunately, when we use the word *work*, we usually refer to paid employment. For most people, however, this is only part of their daily work, and for others like Liz, their work doesn't include any paid work at all. Sadly, the value of "paid" work is generally assumed to be of much greater importance than any unpaid tasks or roles we perform. This is not how it should be.

A CULTURAL DILEMMA

When it comes to defining work in our culture, we have a real problem. The word *work* has become almost totally defined by paid employment. When we meet someone for the first time, and that person asks what we "do," we usually reply, "I'm a builder" or "I work for Telecom." Instinctively, we know that the question really means, "What is your paid employment?"

More than anything else, the matter of "employment" defines who we are in the eyes of our culture. Yet, as Christians, do we really believe that? Surely there are more important ways of identifying *who* we are. And what about those who, for whatever reason, don't have a paid job? They will tell you (and if you are such a person, you know this only too well) that this question is disturbingly awkward to answer. Worse, it raises fearful questions about your own self-worth, which many people are unable to face.

DEFINING *WORK* BIBLICALLY

This narrow view of work is problematic when we come to examining the Scriptures. The biblical writers lived in a tightly connected and closely integrated society. In their lives, home and employment, relationships and activities were not separate spheres but had real and obvious everyday connections. Our fragmented and highly compartmentalized world doesn't connect well with that society. If we are to read the Scriptures with an understanding of their full meaning, then we need to develop a much broader, holistic definition of work. Here are a couple of examples of people attempting to do this.

Paul Marshall defines *work* as "human activity designed to accomplish something that is needed, as distinct from activity that is satisfying in itself."[1] John Stott suggests that *work* is "the expenditure of energy (manual or mental or both) in the service of others, which brings fulfillment to the worker, benefit to the community and glory to God."[2] There are obviously a number of ways to nail down what we mean by *work*. Not getting hung up on the details, let's simply note that by seeing *work* as much broader than paid employment, we will understand more thoroughly the biblical references to this topic.

Am I working when I read to my daughter in bed? In a sense, I am. I may find it dull and unstimulating, or pleasant and fulfilling. Either way there's a degree of expended energy involved, and it's an important task in the overall goal of raising and discipling my daughter. What about when I attend a school or community committee? Or when my elderly neighbor needs help with her groceries? Or when a friend has just lost a brother through death and needs someone to be there, to sit with him and listen? You bet! Some may be instinctive responses to people in need, while others may be quite deliberately planned; some may seem effortless and "self-rewarding," while others may be a real chore and require major application—but all of these "tasks" are work.

Students work. Superannuates work. Stay-at-home parents work. "Unemployed" people work. We all work. It's the dominant activity of our everyday lives, consuming the majority of our waking hours. Whether or not we get paid for the task is somewhat irrelevant, at least insofar as whether it counts for work. So over the next few pages, when you read the word *work*, make sure you include all productive activities you engage in on a weekly basis.

||||||||||||||||||||||||||||||||||||||||||||UP CLOSE & PERSONAL

1. Which of the five profiles above do you identify with? (You might like to read them through again and underline anything that sounds like you.)

2. What conflicts are you aware of at the moment between your church life and your everyday activities?

3. As a group, try to come up with a definition of *work* that satisfies everyone.

4. When someone asks you what you "do," what do you usually say? Is it difficult or easy for you to answer this question when asked? What are practical ways you could change the way you think and talk about *work*, to incorporate a wider definition of it?

5. If Jesus joined you each week and worked alongside you in your Monday-to-Saturday activities (remember: he was a tradesman himself), would that make any difference to the way you do your daily work? If so, what sort of difference?

EXERCISE

Make a list of all the tasks you do and the roles you play in a standard week. Be sure to cover *all* your paid and unpaid tasks—including domestic chores, community and church involvement, parenting, and so on. (Note: Subsequent exercises in this book will regularly refer back to this list, so make sure you take time to be as comprehensive as possible.)

- Which of these tasks do you normally refer to as *work*? Why these ones and not the others on the list?

- Choose two tasks from your list that you enjoy most and two you enjoy least. Why is there a difference?

- Share this list with your group members. As people read their lists, take care to notice the diversity of their activities.

WORK AND THE BIBLE

1

God's Creative Work

How Work Began

Where did work come from? Who invented it? Is it just a negative consequence of the Fall? Perhaps it is a punishment by God on us sinful humans? There are certainly times when we all feel that way—particularly when work seems so hard and frustrating. The biblical reality, however, is quite different.

GOD IS A WORKER

The Bible leaves us with the unmistakable message that right from the beginning of time work is good. We see this in Genesis 1, which is really an account of work—embarked on by God and obviously satisfying to him. As Eugene Peterson writes:

> The Bible begins with the announcement, "In the beginning God created." Not "sat majestic in the heavens." He created. He did something. He made something. He fashioned heaven and earth. The week of creation was a week of work.[1]

An interesting exercise is to read through the first two chapters of Genesis, highlighting all the verbs that describe activities engaged in by God or others. You'll soon discover the breadth of God's work habits and the range of his creative genius.

Think of the fun God must have had dreaming up and making stuff that never existed before. What a wild imagination! God is intensely innovative and his development of Planet Earth (to say nothing of the rest of the universe) is thoroughly groundbreaking. In making the land and sea, a million varieties of living creatures, night and day, trees and plants by the score, and much more, God shows himself to be the ultimate trailblazer, a master craftsperson.

Now here's an important point: If being creative is core to who God is, then it's clear that God did not stop creating after Genesis 1 and 2. His creative energies are still being applied. For example, we know from scientists that the universe continues to grow. There are galaxies being added all the time. And we must assume there are countless other ways his creativity is being expressed, even as you read this—such as all the totally unique babies being born around the world right at this minute.

In fact, it's interesting to observe, as Robert Banks notes in his book *God the Worker*, the number of images used throughout Scripture to describe aspects of God's work, such as shepherd, potter/craftsperson, builder and architect, weaver, gardener, farmer, musician and artist.[2] So here in Genesis, right at the beginning of the Bible, we are faced with the truth that God himself is a worker. Purposeful activity is an intrinsic part of God's character and nature.

Work, however, is not the sum total of all that God is or does. Genesis 2:2 tells us that "God . . . on the seventh day rested from all his work." This is not because he exhausted himself, but so he could enjoy what he had created. Rest complements work, and indeed work makes sense only in the light of rest.

CREATION: BORN TO WORK IN PARTNERSHIP WITH GOD

God's creative work tells us much about who he is and what he is like. Although the picture may not be complete, it does give us a glimpse of his character. This is particularly so in God's act of creating men and women—the ultimate expression of his creativity. This is a point well captured by the psalmist in Psalm 139, who congratulates God for making us so wonderfully unique and complex, both inside and out.

In fact, God states in Genesis 1:26, "Let us make mankind in our image, in our likeness." This tells us much about ourselves. We have been made to resemble and reflect who God is. Therefore, because work is part of God's nature, he clearly intends it to be part of ours as well. In other words, we are workers because we are made in the image of a God who works. It's in our genes. Like Father, like sons and daughters; we too need to be engaged in creative and purposeful activities. Deprived of this opportunity, we are robbed of something essential for our well-being. Think how you feel when you have nothing to do and time lies heavy on your hands!

But our involvement in work is not simply for our own benefit. God has a job for us—he wants our help in achieving his purposes. His intention is for us to become his co-workers. God gave Adam and Eve the mandate to *share in his work*. At the very beginning, God was prepared to entrust the garden to humans. (It is interesting to note that God creates Eve to be a helper to Adam. She is to help him fulfill the responsibilities with which God had entrusted him.) Having been "made in God's image," we are called to be God's representatives. We are God's hands and feet, working in partnership with him in his world.

In the Creation narrative of Genesis 1, this is expressed in God's command for us to "fill the earth and subdue it" and to "rule" over all living things. This stewardship role is a call for humans to work *with* God using our abilities, time, and possessions to further God's purposes. Because of this, the value and significance of our work is directly related to how connected it is with God's work.

We find further expressions of this partnership in Genesis 2, in the story about the planting of the garden and the naming of the animals. Here, God is the landscaper who designs the garden and plants trees that are both economically functional ("good for food") and aesthetically pleasing ("pleasing to the eyes"). Clearly, the value of work should not be measured by economic criteria alone.

Then we are told that God placed a person in the garden to "work it and take care of it," to cultivate and to conserve. Thus God's creative work is linked with *our* creativity—a creativity that is designed both to preserve what God has given and to build on it through further creative ventures, using the resources that God has provided. The "working" suggests that we have a role to play in helping prepare things so that the potential for growth God has placed in them can be realized.

In the story of the naming of the animals, we find God creating animals and birds and then parading them past the man so he can name them. The man is invited to add his creativity to God's. "Whatever the man called each living creature, that was its name." Given the significance of naming in Hebrew culture, clearly the man is delegated both real responsibility and great freedom.

CONCLUSIONS

In summary then, we can say that:

- Work is good. If God does it, then it must be acceptable.
- We are meant to be God's co-workers and help bring about God's purposes.
- God intends for us to share responsibility and exercise our creativity.
- The value and significance of our work is directly dependent on its connection to God's work.

1. Read through the first two chapters of Genesis, highlighting all the verbs (the "doing" words) that describe God's activities. Make a list of them and then describe the range of God's work.

2. Now read through the first two chapters of Genesis again, highlighting all the words that talk about human work. How are these tasks related to God's work? What similarities or connections can you see between these tasks and the work you do?

3. Is *all* work good?

EXERCISE

Look back over the list of work—tasks and roles—you made at the end of the Introduction.

- Can you see any of the activities engaged in by God reflected in your work?

- What opportunities do the tasks you undertake give you to be creative?

2

Corrupted Work

What Went Wrong?

Corrupted computer files are a sad reality of digital technology. After working hard to craft a document, it can be devastating to open the file sometime later and discover it is no longer as you created it. A virus has worked its way in, and while you may still be able to decipher the basic shape and outline of the document, it's no longer what it was meant to be.

The story of Genesis is a bit like that. God's vision for his creation—and for humanity—was stunning and beautiful. The first humans must have been in their element. And then . . . disaster! It's no surprise, then, that the damage done in Genesis 3 extends so clearly, and so painfully, into the area of work, even our work today.

> "Cursed is the ground because of you;
> > through painful toil you will eat food from it
> > all the days of your life.
> It will produce thorns and thistles for you,
> > and you will eat the plants of the field.
> By the sweat of your brow you will eat your food
> > until you return to the ground." (Gen. 3:17–19)

Hardly a pleasant prospect. No wonder so many of us avoid spending time in our gardens!

However, the negative impact of the "Great Rebellion" had much wider implications than just growing food. All four fundamental relationships and their connection to our work were significantly corrupted: our relationship with God, with ourselves, with others, and with the rest of creation.

OUR RELATIONSHIP WITH GOD

In the pre-Fall days, Adam and Eve were at one with God the Trinity. Not only did they enjoy absolute intimacy with him but also the tasks he gave them that were full of value and dignity. They worked as partners with God. Consequently, everything in life was sacred, because everything had something of the touch of God on it. Nothing was "disconnected."

Since the Fall, we humans have struggled to discover the connection (and therefore significance) between the work we were commissioned to do and God. Because we rebelled against God, the fulfillment and purpose of our work was seriously corrupted. The problem is that we yearn to work in partnership with God, yet we insist on doing our own thing.

No wonder then that what happens on Sundays is frequently so "unreal" and even irrelevant to our lives during the rest of the week. Many people notice the divide more and more as they grow older. Many have left the church altogether because they couldn't see the point. For them religious activities, especially the "worship service" on Sunday, feels totally out of touch with "real life."

Others of us have lost sight of God's role for us in his world. We may thrive in the "church atmosphere," but we simply "put up" with our paid employment—treating it only as a way to make a buck and get on with "really living" in the company of our fellow believers. Which is worse? Losing touch with the church that God calls, or losing touch with the world God loves?

OUR RELATIONSHIP WITH OURSELVES

The Fall also directly affects our relationship with ourselves. In the early days of creation, Adam and Eve were at peace with themselves, confident in the roles entrusted to them. There was a sense of dignity and fulfillment in being God's co-workers. The work they did was a part of God's blessing and enabled them to flourish.

Now, however, we constantly find ourselves battling to discover where we "fit." This is no longer automatic, and it is hardly surprising that being out of step with God we struggle to find our identity as workers. Tasks don't effortlessly fit our unique mix of motivations, giftings, and temperament. We often even have little understanding of ourselves—how we are made and what tasks are best for us.

How many times do we catch ourselves (or others) saying, "This job is just not me," or "I really like my work, but it would be so much better if I didn't have to do this or that [fill in your task]"? We're rarely satisfied and fulfilled in what we do. Those who richly enjoy their work are very much the exception to the rule—and if they do, they often end up consumed by their work. For too many of us, our work often seems futile or just plain hard work and toil—far from life-giving.

As a result, some of us become compulsive workers, while others find every day a dreary treadmill. Workaholism or meaninglessness—life often seems to oscillate between these two extremes as we desperately search to find the balance. Too often, this confusion dictates the way we value ourselves. Rather than our identity being rooted in our relationships with God and others, it becomes bound up with our work. (We'll look more extensively at these two tendencies in chapter 9, "Work as Worship: Serving Our Ultimate Boss.")

OUR RELATIONSHIP WITH OTHERS

Honesty, transparency, care, and compassion were all marks of relationships before the Fall. Work built friendship and community. Since then, however, our working lives have become contaminated by all sorts of distractions—blame-shifting, power struggles, deceit, greed, dishonesty, selfishness, stress, and the list goes on.

Relationships in our work have been deeply affected, particularly by the lack of trust between people. For it is trust and respect that make up the oil in working relationships. And this trust has been subverted further in recent decades through the economic rationalizing that has taken place to increase productivity. This has often resulted in the erosion of trust between employees and employers. Unfortunately, in this less secure environment employees frequently find themselves competing with one another to bolster their own job security. As these pressures increase, workplace relationships come under more stress. Trying to get along with a diverse group of people is challenging enough without these additional pressures.

This problem of relationships complicates the issue of work. Often our discontent is not with the job itself, but with the people we have to work alongside! Our personal struggles and the interpersonal conflicts that inevitably follow are yet another result of the Great Rebellion.

OUR RELATIONSHIP WITH THE REST OF CREATION

The Creation story speaks of a world where harmony between created beings was the norm. In this environment, humans were commissioned to care for and steward the animal life and natural resources. The Fall dramatically disturbed this equilibrium. Our greed and ignorance have led to all manner of ecological disasters—along with the mistreatment of countless other living species.

The result is seen everywhere. Pollution haunts our communities. We waste limited resources. When we strip the land of trees for farming, we find the results are erosion and floods. When we introduce exotic species, we upset the balance of nature in a different climate. When we factory farm, overfish, and generally treat the birds, sea life, and animals with whom we share the Earth with contempt, the damage is immense. We were commanded to conserve and cultivate, but too often we abuse and exploit.

FINDING THE BALANCE

Much (though not all) of the damage created by sin is repairable, particularly if people have the will to cooperate with others and with God. Nevertheless, this does produce a built-in tension between frustration and satisfaction. There is the potential for work to be deeply satisfying, but also for it to be full of despair and futility. We'll look more extensively at this in chapter 5, "Futile Work: Struggle and Frustration."

We should be neither resigned to toilsome work nor triumphalistic. It's only too easy to sideline ourselves from the rest of our fellow workers, fooling ourselves that we don't have any problems. This form of super-spirituality can lead us to understate the ongoing struggles we all go through as we try to discover meaning in what we do.

IIIIIIIIIIIIIIIIIIIIIIIIIIIIIIIIIIIIIIIIIUP CLOSE & PERSONAL

1. How has the Fall (or Great Rebellion) impacted your work (think about more than just paid employment)? For example, how disconnected is your faith from your work? What about your Sunday/Monday connection?

2. If you could change one thing about your employment, what would it be?

3. How dependent are you on work for your sense of self-worth? If you were suddenly unemployed, how would you cope? What other areas of your present life would give you a feeling of self-esteem? Are there other areas you should seriously cultivate in order to balance your life?

4. How much stress do you feel is caused in your place of work by poor relationships? In what ways does this impact your capacity to do your tasks well?

5. What examples can you think of where greed, blame-shifting, deceit, dishonesty, selfishness, power struggles, or lack of thoughtfulness for others have been evident in your workplace?

6. What factors foster trust and respect between people in a workplace? Can you think of particular examples where there has been a breakdown of trust and respect between people? What difference did this make?

7. If you work in a relatively warm and friendly environment, what do you think are the key ingredients that make it that way? Do good relationships influence productivity? Or are there advantages in competition between workers?

EXERCISE

Refer back to the list you made at the end of the introduction.

- How well do you feel the tasks you are asked to do fit your own particular mix of personality/temperament/ giftings?

- What tasks do you revel in, and which ones do you find unappealing or frustrating?

- Are there any aspects of your work or work environment where creation is abused or exploited in some way?

3

GOD'S TRANSFORMING WORK

A Restoration Job

A good friend of Wayne's is a classic hoarder, but with a difference. He takes great delight in recycling used engine oil and discarded plastic containers, producing in the process new objects, items, gizmos, gadgets, and doohickeys! His creativity and vision are amazing. Material (most of which is not biodegradable) that would normally end up in the garbage is "redeemed." This person's industry transforms some items into things of beauty and others into articles of usefulness. In a small way, he is participating in God's intention to redeem his creation.

Redeem is a word that early Christian writers quickly adopted. In its original sense (the Latin verb *redimere*; one of its forms is *redemptum*), it means "to buy back, release, ransom" and is used of prisoners, slaves, and so forth. It is the perfect metaphor for the way God saved us while we were still sinners, through the sacrifice of Jesus.

Many of us have been taught that redemption refers only to people's "souls." But the Bible makes it clear that God is in the business of putting right the *whole* cosmos. As Paul states in Colossians 1:18–22:

He [Jesus] was supreme in the beginning and—leading the resurrection parade—he is supreme in the end. From beginning to end he's there, towering far above everything, everyone. So spacious is he, so roomy, that everything of God finds its proper place in him without crowding. Not only that, but all the broken and dislocated pieces of the universe—people and things, animals and atoms—get properly fixed and fit together in vibrant harmonies, all because of his death, his blood that poured down from the cross.

You yourselves are a case study of what he does. At one time you all had your backs turned to God, thinking rebellious thoughts of him, giving him trouble every chance you got. But now, by giving himself completely at the Cross, actually *dying* for you, Christ brought you over to God's side and put your lives together, whole and holy in his presence. (*The Message*)

God's program for restoration is already in place. He intends to transform and redeem everything and everyone—all that he brought into being. God wants to bring order out of chaos, resolve conflict and restore relationships, and work for justice and just solutions in all situations.

In fact, God's redeeming work involves the restoration of all four foundational relationships: with him, with ourselves, with each other, and with the rest of creation. Paul also addresses this in his letters to the Romans (8:18–23) and Ephesians (1:9–12). God has no intention of disposing with Planet Earth after this age comes to a close. Like Wayne's friend, he's just not the throwaway type! Everything we do to counter or reverse the effects of the Fall is a participation in God's redeeming and transforming work, and looks forward to the completion of that work. We are invited to become agents and examples of Christ the Redeemer.

HOW SHOULD THIS AFFECT OUR EVERYDAY WORK?

As we have already seen, work is a part of our humanity especially impacted by the Fall. It figures, then, that it is also one of the things most in need of redemption. Some industries and professions leap to mind—the selling of cars or real estate or insurance, the spheres of politics, law, and advertising. However, what about the more "caring" fields of work such as education, health, and social work? Do they also need redemption? Absolutely. A curious feature of present-day Christian life is the way we treat certain industries or parts of society as "unclean," as if we dare not get involved in them. We fear that our reputation might be tainted if we come too close—much like the Pharisees whom Jesus criticized so severely.

Yet without getting our hands dirty and taking some risks, how can we hope to effectively partner with God in his work of redemption? Jesus showed no such squeamishness when he purposefully involved himself with the undesirables of his time. His deliberate practice of associating with them earned him the accusation of being "a glutton and a drunkard, a friend of tax collectors and sinners" (Luke 7:34).

Yes, the real estate sales industry (for example) is often highly unredeemed. Maybe that's a good reason for Christians who have an authentic kingdom vision to get involved in it. The more unredeemed an area of society may be, the bigger the difference we might be able to make.

WHAT KIND OF TRANSFORMATION IS REQUIRED?

Redemption, though, from what? The best way to get a perspective on this is to think about any area of work and imagine what it would look like if God accomplished his will, both on the macro and the micro level.

For example, when Wayne worked as a school trustee, he was responsible (along with a group of others) for the governance of an elementary school. The kind of questions he found himself grappling with were ones such as: What might this school look like if God was able to make all the changes he wanted? How would it affect the attitudes of the staff and students, the "culture" of the school, the physical environment, the values and educational philosophy, teacher relationships, involvement of the wider community, the learning process, the sense of fulfillment of staff, and times of celebration within the school community?

The vision of a school community being redeemed by God inspired Wayne, as a parent and a trustee, helping him see where he might put his efforts. Of course, he had to learn to recognize the limitations of his "power" or influence to work for change. There were many factors outside his orbit—attitudes within the community, government policies and funding, quality of management and staff, and so on. But this didn't need to lead to discouragement, for there was much change that Wayne, in conjunction with God and others, could work toward. It was, after all, *God's* work of redemption. Wayne was just one of God's partners!

In all our roles and tasks, we need to be prayerfully discerning. Let's think about how we can (among other things) do the following:

- Steward resources well

- Serve others with joy

- Employ God-given creativity

- Witness to God's truth

- Tell the truth and encourage habits such as honesty

- Bring healing, understanding, and reconciliation

- Build community and promote peace and harmony

- Preserve and conserve

- Work for justice and peacemaking

- Nurture and encourage others' gifts and character development

These are all clear expressions of the character and ongoing work of God.

REDEEMING OUR OWN ATTITUDES

However, it's not just what we put our hands to that requires transformation. Clearly, before we attempt to work with God toward redeeming the areas of society we are involved in, we need to begin by allowing our own attitudes and values to be redeemed.

Do we really see the potential for good in what we do? Perhaps we should begin further back and ask if we see any value and purpose in it at all. Many Christians regard paid employment as no more than an opportunity to earn money so they can do "important other stuff." Others, while accepting the need for honesty, see the value of a job mainly in terms of the opportunity to "witness" to their non-Christian workmates or customers.

We do not want to diminish the significance of values such as honesty nor undermine the importance of witness. God is all for these. We believe, however, that God intends to do more than simply "save souls." It is also his plan to transform those souls, *and* the world they dwell in. More to the point, he wants to transform *us*. And he wants us to be his partners in transforming his world. (This is a matter we'll look at in more depth in chapter 10.)

It is often our attitude toward our tasks and roles that limits God. We are too ignorant of God's plans for his cosmos. Since we put little effort into thinking about his intentions for both us and the work we do, it's no wonder that little connecting and transforming really takes place.

Try adopting the attitude that there is value and significance in every one of our roles and tasks. They are part of God's agenda for both us and his wider kingdom. God will use our involvement to transform us and others and redeem the circumstances. He uses them to transform our attitudes, values, expectations, and relationships. Our gifts and abilities can be stretched, our character refined, vision enlarged, and new possibilities discovered.

LIMITS TO OUR ROLE

We're not suggesting that each of us can hope to transform a whole industry or area of society by ourselves. Paid employees, for example, are often more limited in what they can change than employers.

Even so, we often underestimate our ability to make a significant difference in our small corner of the world. The data entry worker may not by herself be a force to be reckoned with in redeeming the banking industry, but she certainly has an opening to help grow community in the office, inspire others with her acts of compassion and love, push for better working conditions, build strong and trusting relationships between management and staff, and speak the truth in love. That's a whole lot of challenge for anyone's working week!

So, while not all of us can bring about change on the macro level, we most certainly can at the micro. Unfortunately, few Christians are challenged or inspired about their role in either, resulting in many missed opportunities! Often it's because we struggle to have a vision for what God *could* do through us.

For example, a truck driver may easily belittle his own trade, wondering what significance there is in trucking frozen goods from one place to another. But the truth is that transporting goods to where they are needed is a critical service. Countries without a good transport infrastructure are plagued by shortages, famine, and suffering.

That, however, is just the beginning. If he thinks through his daily work, our truck driver may also be able to see the value in driving courteously, driving efficiently to conserve fuel, expressing God's care and love in the way he relates to people during the day, raising ethical issues with management such as accidentally unfrozen food that's resold, and so on. This is not simply an exercise to help the truck driver feel better about his work. Rather, it helps make sense of how our daily tasks fit into God's call, how what *we* do contributes to God's work of sustaining and redeeming the world.

Or think of parents. The task of parenting is a wonderful opportunity both for the discipling of children and for the parents' own growth. What is God's intention for family life, and for the development of children and teenagers? How should that change the way that the family relates, is disciplined (parents too!), performs duties, celebrates, and has fun together? What can we do to give our children the best spiritual, emotional, and cultural growth? How can we prepare them to follow Christ and to make responsible decisions for themselves? How can we encourage them to grow in personal wholeness and in relationships—knowing that this will dramatically improve their roles as people and eventually as parents themselves? These are just some of the issues of what we might call "redemptive parenting."

We hope these examples help you gain a glimpse of the immense possibilities in working with God. When we capture a vision of the breadth and depth of the transformation God wants to bring, it will make a huge difference in how we work. We'll come back to this important matter of redemption in chapter 10.

THE END/COMPLETION

So what's God's "endgame" in all this? It's that his work of redemption will be completed. Everything and everyone will eventually be as God intended. This raises an interesting question or two. What, then, will the role of work be in the renewed earth? And what does the Bible mean when it talks about eternal rest?

At first glance, we might think of *rest* as simply refraining from work. But perhaps that is primarily because of the "toil factor" that exists as a result of the Fall. If work has been tainted by the appearance of sin, then we may feel we regularly need to escape it! The real function of rest in our lives is to help us recover from times of toil and to prepare us for further work. Rest and recreation (or re-creation) are positive ideas, restoring us when used appropriately but undermining us when overindulged in. (We'll look closer at the role of rest in chapter 6.)

The picture most of us have of the afterlife involves permanent inactivity, reinforced by images of a nonstop church service or even an endless feast. There are, however, indications that the eternal rest we are promised *will* involve work. For example, Isaiah, in writing about the new heavens and new earth, says:

> "They will build houses and dwell in them;
>> they will plant vineyards and eat their fruit. . . .
> They will not labor in vain . . .
>> for they will be a people blessed by the Lord." (Isa. 65:21, 23)

Here we are given a brief glimpse of a much more active and fulfilling eternity—not the passive role we are traditionally taught to associate with life beyond the grave. It is work, but work of a quite different kind.

While it's true that the Scriptures contain only brief references to work in the next life, think again about the nature of God. The need to create is hardwired into us, because that is how God is. The need to extend ourselves and to achieve, to improve conditions and to perfect our surroundings—these are an integral and essential part of who we are, made in God's image. The commission in the Genesis story to "work and take care"—to manage God's creation—remains. We can be confident that work will continue to be part of our lives and that whatever work God challenges us with will be supremely invigorating and energizing. Isn't this an encouragement to grow and prepare ourselves for that future here and now, in our present work? May God grant us the vision and courage to partner with him in bringing about transformation in this life. For it is a taste of things to come.

‖‖‖‖‖‖‖‖‖‖‖‖‖‖‖‖‖‖‖‖‖‖‖‖‖‖‖‖‖‖‖‖‖‖‖UP CLOSE & PERSONAL

1. Why do you think we often have such a truncated or reduced understanding of "redemption"? Are there other biblical words or concepts that might help enlarge our understanding of what needs to be transformed?

2. Are there any industries/occupations that you think are unredeemable? Make a list of them and then explain your reasons for thinking this way.

3. What industries do you think it would be particularly challenging for Christians to work in and attempt to transform? Why?

4. Take some time to read Isaiah 65:17–25 (Isaiah's description of the new creation). What impacts you most about this?

EXERCISE

Look back over your list of tasks and roles at the end of the introduction. Identify the ones that offer you the opportunity to:

- Steward resources well

- Serve others with joy

- Employ God-given creativity

- Witness to God's truth

- Tell the truth and encourage habits such as honesty

- Bring healing, understanding, and reconciliation

- Build community, and promote peace and harmony

- Preserve and conserve

- Work for justice and peacemaking

- Nurture and encourage others' gifts and character development

List features of your weekly work that are personally enriching to you.

4

God's Maintenance Work

Redeeming the Mundane

Wayne's upstairs home office has a splendid vista looking out over trees to the hills beyond. And when he goes downstairs, the view is even better—a backyard full of beautiful gardens, trees, and grass. He often marvels at the creative genius of God and his co-workers (such as his wife, Jill!) who have created such beauty and inspiration.

But nothing ever stays the same. The splendor of the view also reminds him of tasks that need doing—lawns to mow, trees to prune, fences to rebuild or paint, a house to wash, and gardens to weed. If he could just get the benefit of the great surroundings without having to constantly tidy up, then everything would be perfect! This, of course, is the reality of living in God's created world. A world full of beauty and wonder is also a world of both growth and decay. Maintenance is part of the deal.

And that's true for God's tasks as well. Sometimes we assume that God's work ended the day the cosmos—his great creative masterpiece—was finished. But his responsibility did not stop there. He is still hard at work sustaining life in our universe. Much like the work required to maintain a beautiful garden, God's ongoing attention is required. He is not some remote creator who has lost interest in his universe.

GOD'S "PROVIDENCE"

For many centuries Christians have used the word *providence* to describe this involvement. Simply put, the universe continues to depend on the continuing touch of its Creator every moment to maintain its existence. If God stopped working, then our universe would disintegrate. His providence is what allows our world to continue. Alec Motyer, in his exploration of the meaning of Isaiah 42:5–6 in *The Prophecy of Isaiah*, puts it this way: "The power which called everything into being keeps it in being."[1]

The Bible backs this up. For example, Hebrews 1:3 states that the Son is "sustaining all things by his powerful word," while Paul comments in Colossians 1:17, "In him [the Son] all things hold together." Peter expresses this same thought somewhat differently when he writes, "By the same word the present heavens and earth are reserved for fire, being kept for the day of judgment" (2 Pet. 3:7). Job 34:14 and Psalm 104:29 also say that if God ceased to breathe his life into us, then we would immediately return to dust. A sobering thought. Of course, this activity of God's does not appear nearly as dramatic as those initial acts of creation. This is more like God's housekeeping work. Nevertheless, without his continuing involvement in this way, life would cease, chaos would reign, and the universe would disintegrate.

Although this sustaining work is different from the redeeming work we considered in the previous chapter, they inevitably overlap. Redeeming work seeks to transform a negative situation and make it better, never settling for the status quo. Sustaining work maintains life by preserving the status quo. Both are important.

PRACTICING GOD'S PRESENCE

One of the main ways God maintains life on this planet is through our work—tasks such as cleaning, painting, repairing, even putting out the rubbish! These often boring, routine chores hardly seem like spiritual tasks. But they are—even if practicing the presence of God in the midst of the mundane does not come automatically. We all find it easy to see God at work in miraculous events, but less so in everyday ones. As a result, we end up with a much-reduced vision of God and his work. And sadly, it's also a very limited vision of the significance of our own daily work. We fail to see it through God's eyes.

Cultivating, growing, picking, preparing, cooking, parenting, nurturing, educating, collecting, counting, administering, distributing, transporting, testing, preserving, cleaning, serving—all of these activities, and many more, are examples of our sustaining work. They are, therefore, part of God's maintenance work too. These tasks all have value and significance. If we don't mow the lawn, repair the fence, paint the house, and trim the trees, our backyard will soon become overgrown and our house will rot and decay. This work is an important part of our roles as stewards of God's creation. And it's only as we begin to recognize the roles these tasks play in sustaining life that we are able to infuse them with the dignity they deserve.

If we're really going to recapture a sense of God in the midst of the mundane, then we will need to develop a new kind of everyday spirituality and a new sense of awe in the ordinary. We'll need to recognize God at work in every set of circumstances, with no part of life untouched by his presence or excluded from his purposes.

GOD'S WORK OF RESTRAINT

There's another aspect to God's sustaining work, which has to do with restraining evil in our world. We looked briefly at the impact of the Fall on the world of work in a previous chapter. But part of God's work is also to hold evil in check and to limit the extent of harm and destruction it causes.

Here's where the command of Jesus to his followers to be salt in the world makes real sense. Salt is a preservative, and its presence enables food to remain good and wholesome for considerable periods of time. As God's co-workers, this is one of our roles. Some ways in which our work is linked to this restraining aspect of God's work include exercising discipline, developing legal restraints and rules, monitoring and enforcing laws, peacemaking, and holding things together when they threaten to fall apart.

To some people, the extent of evil seems already too awful to contemplate and actually becomes a barrier to belief in the goodness of God. For others, however, the mere fact that life continues with as many good experiences as we enjoy is witness to the restraining power of God at work in a world that would otherwise disintegrate. The chaos in our world would be so much worse without God's restraining hand.

ⅢⅢⅢⅢⅢⅢⅢⅢⅢⅢⅢⅢⅢⅢⅢⅢⅢⅢⅢⅢⅢⅢⅢⅢUP CLOSE & PERSONAL

1. How do you understand *providence*?

2. In what ways do you see God working now to sustain his creation?

3. Make a list of as many tasks and occupations as you can think of where the sustaining role of work is foremost.

4. In what ways do you see your personal work connected to God's sustaining work?

5. In what ways can you see your work and involvement as a preservative (that is, salt)?

6. What do you think about this statement from the last paragraph above? "To some people, the extent of evil seems already too awful to contemplate and actually becomes a

barrier to belief in the goodness of God. For others, however, the mere fact that life continues with as many good experiences as we enjoy is witness to the restraining power of God at work in a world that would otherwise disintegrate."

EXERCISE

Refer back to the list of tasks and roles you made at the end of the introduction.

- Mark the ones that are primarily maintenance tasks.

- Now mark the ones that are mundane tasks.

- Which tasks have you marked twice?

Spend some time reflecting on how you can value these the same way God does. How might you be able to view these tasks as spiritual exercises?

5

FUTILE WORK

Struggle and Frustration

The biblical writers are very realistic in their appraisal of what work can be like as a result of the Fall. Take Ecclesiastes, for example:

> I hated all the things I had toiled for under the sun, because I must leave them to the one who comes after me. And who knows whether that person will be wise or foolish? Yet they will have control over all the fruit of my toil into which I have poured my effort and skill under the sun. This too is meaningless. So my heart began to despair over all my toilsome labor under the sun. For a person may labor with wisdom, knowledge and skill, and then they must leave all they own to another who has not toiled for it. (Eccl. 2:18–21)

> And I saw that all toil and all achievement spring from one person's envy of another. This too is meaningless, a chasing after the wind. (Eccl. 4:4)

Depressing stuff. Unfortunately, work can be incredibly tedious, frustrating, and meaningless. And it is so for countless numbers of us. If we're honest with ourselves, who hasn't at some time asked the question, "What on earth am I doing this for?" Deep down, all of us want to be reassured that our toil is going to count for something in the long term.

Meaninglessness can drive us to despair, and ultimately to insanity. The frequently told story of a Nazi concentration camp bears that out. A shrewd and sadistic camp commandant had a group of men toil all day long to shift a huge pile of dirt from one spot in the camp to another. The next day they were ordered to repeat the process—in reverse. On this went, day after day. The sheer meaninglessness of the task quickly wore those able-bodied prisoners down. It deeply affected their psyches and eventually destroyed their reason to live. Often, unfortunately, we inflict this tragic fate on ourselves. Some of the world's richest men and women have ended life despairing of all they have achieved. One even summed it up by saying, "I am the most miserable man on earth!"

Or what about Ramses II, perhaps the greatest of the ancient Egyptian pharaohs? His building program was one of the biggest and most extravagant of any ruler's. The British poet Shelley wrote a poem about him, titled "Ozymandias" (another name for Ramses). This is what remains of all that Ramses invested his life in:

I met a traveller from an antique land
Who said: Two vast and trunkless legs of stone
Stand in the desert. Near them on the sand,
Half sunk, a shattered visage lies, whose frown
And wrinkled lip and sneer of cold command
Tell that its sculptor well those passions read
Which yet survive, stamped on these lifeless things,
The hand that mocked them and the heart that fed;
And on the pedestal these words appear:
"My name is Ozymandias, king of kings:
Look on my works, ye Mighty, and despair!"
Nothing beside remains. Round the decay
Of that colossal wreck, boundless and bare,
The lone and level sands stretch far away.

ASKING THE DIFFICULT QUESTIONS

Reading Ecclesiastes forces us to ask the difficult questions about the meaning of life—and of work. The writer, reflecting on his experience, has come to the conclusion that so much is frustrating and meaningless without a God-centered worldview. Within his depressing honesty, there is clearly a warning for readers on the subject of work.

INVESTING IN PEOPLE, NOT THINGS

The first warning is not to count on building monuments that will endure forever. Neither great wealth nor great possessions will last the distance. The only worthwhile investment is people. If the writer of Ecclesiastes is indeed Solomon, then he certainly was writing from personal experience. Like Ramses, Solomon put a huge amount of energy into extensive building programs, and his wealth grew enormously throughout his reign. In Ecclesiastes 2:10–11, he concludes:

> My heart took delight in all my labor, and this was the reward for all my toil. Yet when I surveyed all that my hands had done and what I had toiled to achieve, everything was meaningless, a chasing after the wind; nothing was gained under the sun.

CONTENTMENT AND DISSATISFACTION

The second warning is to not look for easily quantifiable value in every task we do and every moment we spend. Solomon's counsel is very down to earth. In Ecclesiastes 3, he suggests that God's people will always live with a tension. God has put eternity in our hearts, so we are always hungry to know more than this life can ever offer. We want to enjoy an intimacy with

God and with one another, and a satisfaction in our work in the here and now that we cannot fully achieve. To be sure, in God's presence we will at last find such total fulfillment, but in this life we must accept the tension. We will never be able to figure out exactly what God is up to or why he seems to choose such roundabout ways to accomplish his purposes. These are mysteries we must learn to live with.

And so is the tension between contentment and discontentment—particularly in our work, where the conflict between our ideals and reality seems most intense. But Solomon suggests (in Ecclesiastes 3:14) that this is just how God intends it. This is what makes us dependent on him. This is why we have to rely on his grace. If it was easy, then we would start thinking that we'd accomplished it by ourselves. It may be frustrating that it's all so mysterious, but it's designed that way in order to push us back to reliance on God—and to remember his presence in the midst of the mundane.

SERVING OTHERS

The third warning in Ecclesiastes is that if we work only for ourselves, it will seem pointless in the end. We have been made for community, and to serve others. "A cord of three strands is not quickly broken" (Eccl. 4:12).

In our present society, money and status are held up as important motivating factors and a reason why students should apply themselves to the demands of study. But the writer of Ecclesiastes says it is better to settle for a handful of goods and live with contentment than be forever working feverishly for two handfuls. We will discover—too late—that it just isn't worth it.

Jesus, too, cautioned against rampant self-focused ambition. In Luke 12, he tells the parable of the rich fool—a wealthy landowner who, in a fit of greed and selfishness, decided to build bigger barns to house his bumper crop, so that he could enjoy the "good life" without ever having to work again. God, seeing his heart, labels him a fool and takes his life away. Eugene Peterson translates Jesus's punch line as, "That's what happens when you fill your barn with Self and not with God" (Luke 12:21, *The Message*). Of this parable, Craig Evans writes:

> The man is implicitly selfish. He does not see this abundance as an opportunity to help those needing food. Rather, he hoards his plenty and then relaxes under the assumption that his troubles are over. Herein lies his folly. The day will come, often sooner than expected, when all persons will have to stand before God and give an account. All that the fool will have to show for his life will be bigger barns crammed with food, food that will be enjoyed by others now that he is dead. Rather than giving away his surplus, and so laying up treasure in heaven, he has selfishly and greedily hoarded his worldly goods with the result that in the end he does not even benefit from them.[1]

There is real significance in work that serves others and God. This is what we were made for. Our culture's promotion of the self-centered good life is a dead-end and will bring no lasting satisfaction.

Conversely, when we seize the opportunities presented to us every day to serve others and build friendship through our work, genuine fulfillment can come. Each task. Each transaction. Every relationship. All these can become expressions of care and concern for others. If you are in touch with God, every action can become a living reminder of his love and grace for others.

IN SUMMARY

The book of Ecclesiastes certainly invites us to be honest about the frustrations and struggles we experience. But we shouldn't make the mistake of letting those frustrations grow out of proportion. We shouldn't think that God is not with us *in* our struggles. For quite the opposite is true. *Because* God is in our struggles, *that's* why we feel the tension. At the very moment we're tempted to run, God calls us to stand. We need to be awake to see God at work in places where we were previously blind to his presence.

Our daily work is part of our service for God. And our daily work (as we'll talk more about in chapter 9) is part of our worship of God—for worship is not something we do only on Sunday. It is our gift—of ourselves and of our creativity—to our Father.

With penetrating skepticism, Ecclesiastes probes the underside of life and exposes the futility of so much the world encourages us to pursue. But the aim is not to leave us depressed and discouraged. Rather, it should help us live with a new liberty—released from the anxiety and fears so many of us have when we are preoccupied with the need to build bigger barns, or to make more money, or to push harder for promotion.

|||||||||||||||||||||||||||||||||||||||||||||UP CLOSE & PERSONAL

1. What kind of "legacy" are you hoping to leave with those who know you? Are you confident it will stand the test of time?

2. Personal meditation: Reflect on your dreams and ambitions. Are they self-focused or primarily other-directed? Short term or long term?

EXERCISE

Refer back to your list of tasks and roles at the end of the introduction.

- What tasks/work do you find frustrating or meaning-less? Why?

- What tasks/work do you find fulfilling and purposeful? Why?

- How is the work you're engaged in able to serve others?

- In what ways are you investing in other people?

6

RESTING FROM WORK

Taking a Break

What do you think of when you hear the word *rest*? Do you dream of quiet days in a deck chair on a deserted beach? Or perhaps time with family and friends, completely free of the prospect of work?

WHAT THE BIBLE SAYS ABOUT REST

There is much in the Scriptures about rest, almost as much as about work. This is not surprising when you consider that work and rest are two sides of the one coin. You can't have one without the other. And their relationship to each other is modeled in Genesis 1 and 2, within the story of Creation.

> By the seventh day God had finished the work he had been doing; so on the seventh day he rested from all his work. Then God blessed the seventh day and made it holy, because on it he rested from all the work of creating that he had done. (Gen. 2:2–3)

What exactly did God do when he rested? He took a break. He refreshed himself. Was God exhausted so that he needed a rest? Or did he just want to stand back and enjoy what he had made? If we hope to appreciate the worth of something, then we need to take time to enjoy and evaluate it, to catch a glimpse of the big picture and gain a new sense of perspective.

SABBATH

Early in the history of the people of Israel, a "sabbath" was established, based on the example of the Creation story. It was a sign of the covenant. The fourth commandment is one of only two that are given in a positive form: "Remember the Sabbath day by keeping it holy." For the Sabbath was intended by God to be a day of delight, an opportunity to celebrate life and anticipate the future. It was also a day to be set apart, consecrated and dedicated to God.

Like the other commandments, the Sabbath was given in order to keep the people of Israel liberated. The call to "lay down the tools" for one day a week was a discipline intended to break the relentless demands of work. In this sense, it was not so much a "commandment" as a kindness, an example of God's care.

In the Gospels, the Sabbath plays a prominent role. Not surprising, since many of the run-ins Jesus had with the religious authorities sprang out of Sabbath-keeping. The legalism of the day had tied the Sabbath into a highly negative command—with laws against all kinds of trivial activities. This was consistent with the "ethics of avoidance" predominant among the Jews at the time. Their effort to "avoid sin" missed the point of Sabbath rest entirely. The response that Jesus made was to demonstrate mercy, healing, liberation, and restoration. In doing so, he made a dramatic point about the true meaning of the Sabbath. Viewed biblically, the Sabbath is a day of pause, a time of physical rest and renewal, an opportunity for spiritual refreshment. It is a gift from God.

REST, NOT LEISURE

It's important to note the distinction between rest and leisure. Rest and Sabbath are not the same as leisure, though they may certainly overlap. Rest is all about recovering our equilibrium—with God, with ourselves, with others, and with creation. The goal of leisure is personal enjoyment—which may well be a by-product of rest, but not its primary purpose. In fact, leisure can frequently divert us from rest. For many people, it becomes so dependent on frenetic activity that it is just another form of work (like the old "work hard, play hard" maxim), or it becomes so caught up in personal pleasure that there is little room to reconnect with God, our inner selves, or others.

A further complication is the place that consumerism has come to play in our culture. We are constantly bombarded to buy this or that gadget, or take this overseas holiday or that thrill-seeking adventure—as if filling our lives up with more and more pleasurable experiences will somehow lead to greater happiness.

Unquestionably, a Christian needs to discover a place for leisure. However, leisure is not the biblical opposite of work—rest is. For it's as we seek to be renewed and reenergized that we are able to reenter the rhythm of work.

REST IS A DIRTY WORD

In spite of the clear biblical mandate to rest, life is increasingly so full that few people take the time to rest well. Alvin Toffler's prophetic words of the 1970s have been confirmed with remarkable accuracy. Life is dramatically faster now than it was a generation or so ago. Little wonder that the reply I expect most when I ask friends how their week has been is, "I'm just so incredibly busy," or as we say in New Zealand, "Flat stick!"

Why have we allowed the treadmill of life to speed up? Why do we have to live faster and faster, so that our lives seem to be spent just trying to keep pace? No doubt there are many factors, but Gordon MacDonald identifies three key ones in "Rest Stops."

1. Rest Is Not "Productive"

Efficiency and productivity are virtues in our society. And productivity means efficient activity. Our narrow definition of productivity excludes any concept of strengthened relationship, often with unfortunate results. For example, in an efficiency drive in orphanages, staff numbers were reduced. However, it was quickly discovered that when there were not enough staff to handle and hug the babies, the babies simply died.

We can even make ourselves feel guilty if we're not working or being "productive." It's our "productivity" that generally feeds our sense of value and worth. Obviously, rest doesn't fit too well into this equation! It's not productive, it doesn't feed our self-worth, and therefore it's a distraction from what is seen as really important in life.

2. Consumerism

Our culture is fixated on standards of living. We even measure the economy by how much it has grown each year—through the lens of productivity and consumption. Unfortunately, the church has largely bought into this. We are very much products of our society. In the incessant drive to possess more, we have laid a real trap for ourselves. As Gordon MacDonald says,

> The more we want, the more revenue we must produce to get it. The more revenue we must produce, the longer and harder we have to work. So we build larger homes, buy more cars, take on added financial burdens and then find ourselves having to work harder to pay for it all. More work, less rest.[1]

In fact, under these conditions, rest becomes the enemy of work.

3. The Role of Technology

Technology is a wonderful tool. During the original writing of this book, one of us traveled extensively overseas, yet we were able to continue the process of writing and developing the content via a laptop and e-mail, passing the text backwards and forwards around the planet.

It has never been so easy. But the same benefits of technology are also responsible for negative consequences. Smartphones, Wi-Fi, social media, supersonic travel, and the like mean that life is now more hectic than ever before. Virtually everywhere on earth is easily accessible. And our wireless devices have conditioned us to desire continuous "connection." As a result, our work and rest have become so intertwined that many people live most of their week in a confused milieu, unable to concentrate 100 percent on any one activity, constantly distracted by texts, e-mails, and Facebook. Not able to truly work. Not able to truly rest. Far from liberating us, digital technology has enslaved us. It has become our master, and we its servants.

THE CALL TO SIMPLICITY

Somewhere in the midst of all this madness, the gospel calls us to simplicity. Because of the intense pressure exerted to speed up life, to be more "productive," to accumulate more, to experience this or that, to "connect" with everyone, we need to take deliberate action if we're to fight against the current.

All of us live in our own unique circumstances. What we face weekly may very well be different from the challenges you face. All of us, however, can develop habits and routines that help us integrate a work/rest rhythm into our lives. Here are some things we, the writers of this book, have consciously worked at.

Dropping Our Lifestyle Expectations

We've noticed that an enormous amount of stress and effort is given to appeasing our appetite for an increased standard of living. Many of us can actually live on substantially less with little pain: Buying a house in a cheaper area of town and then resisting the desire to "upgrade"; buying a secondhand vehicle that has already depreciated but still has good life in it; settling for mainly secondhand furniture; eating out only occasionally; keeping one's wardrobe to a minimum and wearing clothes till they are well-worn; choosing cheaper forms of entertainment and holidays. These are some of the practices we pursued over the years, and they have significantly reduced the cost of living.

During the years of greatest expense (teenage children!), simplifying our standard of living meant much less financial pressure on us than on many of our friends. We were content to live on a lower income and therefore have more time and energy to give to other matters—including rest.

Walking Rather Than Driving

One of the great technological marvels of our age remains the motor vehicle. It enables many of us to live and work in different communities, and to visit family and friends hundreds of miles away in a short period of time.

Wayne discovered that one of the downsides of his car was that it "upped" the frenetic pace of his life because he was able to get to more places, do more things, and see more people in a day. And city traffic being what it is, his stress levels often increased while in the car.

One of the habits he developed to counter this hectic pace has been to walk where he can or even take public transport. (That's a challenge for him because he's an ex-car dealer!) Walking slows him down. It fills his lungs with air, his nose becomes sensitive to the smell of trees and flowers, he see things that he would otherwise miss at 50km an hour, and he meets people he would normally drive straight past. It gives him time to think, reflect, pray, and relax. Unhurried, he builds a rhythm into his daily life, which makes him better prepared to face the times of busyness.

Not Becoming a Slave to Being "Connected"

Modern inventions have changed the pace of life, and the ubiquitous telephone is one of the clearest examples. Whether landline or cell phone, its insistent ring has become one of the great compulsions of modern life—even more so with the advent of the smartphone.

Wayne bases most of his work from home, which provides him with tremendous advantages: he doesn't have far to commute each day (the traffic is light on the family stairwell!), he keeps his overhead to a minimum, and there is great flexibility in his day for mixing family, friendship, and community responsibilities with employment.

With all upsides, however, there are downsides. One is the accessibility people have to him via the phone. They know he can be reached all times of the day, night, and weekend. The interruption this can cause to family life, let alone rest and recreation, is potentially enormous. He experienced a real breakthrough when he realized he wasn't obliged to answer the phone every time it rang. He did not have to be at the beck and call of everyone.

When he is in need of some time for reflection, rest, or writing, or when we have visitors, he will frequently just let the phone ring. Visitors sometimes get quite unnerved by this, and their faces seem distraught as he continues listening or talking while letting the phone ring. It's as if they want to plead for him to answer it!

Since writing the initial edition of this book, there has been a monumental shift in digital technology—away from the fixed-line telephones, televisions, and stereos, to mobile devices that can go wherever we go. Smartphones, MP3 players, tablets— these are now so dominant in our culture that for many people they act kind of like a prosthetic, an extension of who they are and something they simply can't imagine doing without.

Being wired (or connected) is now a 24/7 experience. Public and private spaces, work and recreation have within a short space of time become thoroughly colonized by screens. Texting, social media, e-mail, downloadable music, movies, video clips,

TV shows, online video games, avatar personas, Skype, and FaceTime—these are the things that fill our lives these days.

While there are some benefits to all this new technology, such constant connectivity has also come at great cost. It has blurred the lines between work, rest, and leisure. It has shortened our attention spans so that most of us are now distracted and have swallowed hook, line, and sinker the lie that "multitasking" is more productive than focusing on a single task. Our relationships at work and at home have become significantly mediated through the media we use—fundamentally changing the very nature of relationships (and, in fact, the way our brains function). As a result, it is becoming harder to find the face-to-face intimacy we all need. Also diminished is our capacity to desire and find genuine solitude and silence, so we can think, pray, reflect, and be renewed by our relationships with God and ourselves.

If we are to be freed from the tyranny of 24/7 connectivity, then most of us will need to take intentional steps to restructure our lives. This will inevitably include carving out spaces and times where we disconnect from the digital world.

THE BIBLICAL RHYTHMS OF LIFE

Not only did God intend for us to experience the regular rhythms of the day (day and night) and week (six days working, one day Sabbath), but there are other laws he laid down for the people of Israel. These include regular "religious festivals" (some lasting several days), the sabbatical year (every seventh year when the land was rested) and the year of Jubilee (the fiftieth year, after seven sets of seven years).

All were intended to structure into the normal schedule of work a balancing rhythm of rest. How we do this in our modern and largely urban context is a personal challenge we all must face. But rest we must, not only because our weary minds and bodies need a "breather," but also because of the constant need to realign ourselves with our Creator and his creation.

‖‖UP CLOSE & PERSONAL

1. If you grew up in the church, describe what part the Sabbath played in your early life. How was it expressed in your family and church context? Then think about how this has changed, both in your understanding and practice of Sabbath.

2. What are some of the changes in our society that now make rest and Sabbath more difficult to keep than, say, thirty years ago?

3. Do you agree with the distinction made between rest and leisure? What forms of leisure do you think are also restful? What type of leisure works against Sabbath?

4. Productivity, consumerism, and technology have been mentioned above as factors that have contributed to the speeding up of life. How have these affected your life? Are there other factors?

5. Spend some time discussing the section on connectivity. Do you agree or disagree? Share your own experiences and reflections of its influence on your life. What kinds of practices might help you to be freed from the tyranny of 24/7 connectivity?

6. Have you ever had the opportunity for a sabbatical? Share your experiences, the lessons you learned, or what you would do differently next time. Discuss creative ways of making space for sabbaticals.

A GIFT FROM GOD: WAYNE'S SABBATH YEAR

I'd had a difficult year. Despite my intense commitment to working with unchurched young people, I was feeling tired. Everything was an effort, and the challenges overwhelmed me. At the end of the year, I sat with other leaders of the organization I served and discussed my predicament. In our conversation, I sensed they meant well, but nothing they said really touched me until one of the leaders—a middle-aged man—spoke about the need for sabbaticals. I had heard the term before, used mainly by my old university lecturers, but it was a foreign concept in the environment of our organization. As he talked, I sensed that—although this wouldn't be the golden answer to my woes—the timing was right to experience a break.

Six months later my wife Jill and I, along with our eight-month-old daughter, found ourselves traveling into the deep south of New Zealand to a small, isolated community. It was the beginning of a four-month adventure that not only restored my sagging energy levels, but more importantly helped set the compass of our lives for the next "season." During those delightful few months, we explored beautiful Fiordland, I worked ten hours a week for a small Baptist fellowship (preaching, leading, and pastoring), we developed rich and deep friendships, and I studied (via a correspondence paper from a North American college). Being enveloped by a caring community and appreciated for what we could contribute to them, having freedom to be a family without the usual demands on our time, studying church history, regaining a sense of spontaneity and of awe—all these elements combined to refresh and renew me. They were some of the key ingredients that made those few months a watershed in my life.

Sabbaticals frequently result in directional changes. I have seen this time and time again with my friends. My sabbatical was just that for me. I came back convinced that my time in youth work was close to an end. I was unaware of what lay ahead, but the direction of my compass was already changing. I discussed this feeling with my fellow workers, and we agreed that I would serve another fifteen months—long enough to pass the baton to others.

As it happened, I ended up going overseas to study at the college from which I had previously done the correspondence paper. A new organization was also in its infancy, and with my colleagues I was able to develop some fresh material and trial new ideas. It was an exciting time. The energy and confidence to explore and change was largely due to the invigoration of the sabbatical.

Sabbaticals Can Be for Everyone

Often I hear people say, "Oh, it's okay for you. You can take time out. But I can't. My boss would never allow me to take an extended time, and he certainly wouldn't pay me for it! You're lucky." Of course, there's truth in these sentiments. Many of us aren't in a position where we can just take a break from our employment. And yet it may not be as impossible as it first appears.

For some, there may be an opportunity to make use of a long service leave. Others may be able to apply for leave without pay, while others may be able to accumulate holidays. Perhaps someone could take alternative low-stress employment for a period. A friend of mine took a year off from youth work and drove buses. "The most enjoyable year of my life," he tells me. What is critical is not so much the length of time, but the intention and purpose of the time.

Even if the ideal of a complete break is not physically possible, there is still the opportunity for opting out of an aspect of our work for a period of time, in order to rest and consider where we are headed. For example, this could involve taking a yearlong sabbatical from church responsibilities or community activities. While this won't provide all the opportunities that a complete break from work does, well-structured time can certainly provide space for plenty of rest, reflection, and reevaluation of priorities.

I realize that the idea of a sabbatical seems risky. It's not easy to abandon the security of our regular life and work commitments.

Yet my experience, and that of several friends, is that it's a richly rewarding exercise. Forgoing taking time off means you'll miss out on a wonderful, refreshing opportunity.

There will often be a cost—lost wages or a lower income. One sabbatical I took resulted in my small business suffering, as I had no one to replace me. And there was some inevitable dislocation in the commitments and relationships I was involved in. But at the end of the day, as with our God-inspired call to take time off each week, we know the cost is worth it—because it's an investment in our mental, physical, emotional and spiritual health, and a refreshment for the next phase of our work.

I'm Not Indispensable

My experience of a sabbatical taught me one invaluable lesson: None of us—despite our gifts, positions of responsibility, or contribution to church and society—is indispensable. God is capable of achieving his purposes without us. I know this might come as a shock to some, but it's true! We are valuable to God, not primarily because of what we can "do" for him, but because of who we are. Sure, he delights in using us, but none of us is indispensable.

This truth has the potential to set us free from our activism and our desperate longing to feel needed. It can cause us to allow our relationships with God, with others, and indeed with ourselves to become genuinely renewed. This, I'm convinced, is one of the great benefits of the weekly Sabbath and of sabbaticals.

7

DUALISTIC WORK

The Spiritual/Secular Split

In the Christian world, there's a perception that we could be doing more for God if only we could free ourselves from the distractions of "the world." The thinking goes something like this:

- I have a simple faith. I distinguish between *spiritual* and *secular*.

- By *spiritual*, I mean anything related to God, anything that's *holy*. This is really the most important sphere of life.

- By *secular*, I'm referring to the everyday matters that have little or nothing to do with God. These are much less important or significant than the *spiritual*.

You can see this clearly in the area of work. "Secular employment" is work "out there in the world." Its main purpose is to allow you to earn some money so you can get on with real life, and, of course, it provides opportunities to *witness* to your non-Christian workmates. Mind you, some forms of secular employment do have what you could call a spiritual value—such as the serving ones of medicine and teaching. But the ideal form of employment is unquestionably "full-time Christian work." That's where you have the opportunity to devote all of your time and energy to the Lord's work, unencumbered by the demands of secular employment. It clearly rates as a much more spiritual occupation than a "normal job."

Perhaps becoming a "full-time Christian worker" is your personal dream, because it's the ultimate way of serving God. Perhaps you long for the day when you're no longer distracted from "real service" for God by having to work for a secular firm, and can give all your time and energy to *ministry*.

How do we define *ministry*? Well, it's anything that deals with the spiritual task. Leading worship on Sunday mornings is ministry. So is teaching Sunday school, leading a home group, preaching, going on an outreach, praying for someone, or being a missionary. To be "in ministry" is to take up the spiritual task of building God's kingdom. Of course, once you have experienced being in ministry, it's difficult to return to secular employment with any degree of passion. Nothing is more significant than doing ministry, which is why full-time Christian workers are highly esteemed in the church—and rightly so. After all, they have sacrificed much (particularly those on the mission field), they're at the forefront of God's work in this world, and they're making a bigger difference for God than those in secular employment.

Ultimately, we think that secular work doesn't really count for much. Things of the world will all pass away. Sure, we can do our best at our daily jobs, but it is what we *do for the Lord* that really counts. Our secular employment is simply a means to an end—or so we think. But is that thinking right? Is certain work more "spiritual" in content? Should it be valued more highly? Many of us certainly live as though it is, but is that biblical? Let's take a look at the light Scripture sheds on the way we view various tasks and jobs.

BIBLICALLY EXAMINING THE SPIRITUAL/ SECULAR SPLIT

"In the Beginning"

This strange habit we have of splitting life into spiritual and secular boxes just doesn't appear in the story of God's creation of work. In fact, as we've already noted, God begins by doing some very "earthy" work himself—creating the universe! God acts as designer, builder, and gardener. Then God takes the bold step of giving to us humans a role in this universe work of his, by commissioning Adam and Eve to be stewards of his creation. Does that sound like a second-rate call? Did Adam really think, "Oh no, I really wanted a more significant role, God. Not a farmer! I mean, isn't there some spiritual task I could do? A priest maybe?"

The Creation account allows no room for a spiritual/secular split. In fact, the writer consistently states, "And it was (very) good," as if to emphasize that God's original intention for his creation was the ideal. Yes, it's tainted and corrupted now, but that is the result of the Fall.

Biblical Characters at Work

So what about the role of people in Scripture? What does this say to us about the spiritual/secular split? For a start, many leading figures in the Bible story were not "professional religious" people. God spoke to them in and through their everyday working lives. Though they were "believers," most were not told to leave their employment in order to follow God's leading—people like Joseph, Daniel, Nehemiah, and Esther, to name a few.

For example, Nehemiah was extolled as a prayerful person, a dynamic and effective leader, even a justice-maker. And he was. But it is rarely pointed out that these attributes belonged to a man whose primary role was to manage a difficult and demanding building project. His strengths were developed within the pressures of his construction deadlines.

The same was true with Joseph, Daniel, and Esther. They were high-level public servants in somewhat anti-Jewish environments. Consequently, they had to struggle through what it meant to serve as representatives of a religious minority, working in an environment that routinely involved worship of foreign gods. Their worldview was substantially different from that of their work colleagues and of the surrounding culture (which is no doubt how many Christians feel today).

These examples (among many others) help us see that the Bible gives little evidence of a secular/spiritual split. The Hebrew worldview was a much more integrated one than that of the Greeks. Involvement in the marketplace didn't disqualify people from undertaking significant tasks. Quite the opposite, in fact.

Jesus

What about Jesus? Did he consider certain types of work better than others? Perhaps he viewed his many years as a carpenter as just "fill-in" time, until he was ready to engage in "public ministry"? Certainly that's the way many people seem to interpret the life of Jesus. But it hardly seems consistent with what we know of him. For God himself, in human form, to spend the majority of his adult years engaged in carpentry speaks volumes for the value of such tasks. Even as a traveling "rabbi," Jesus hardly played by the rules of his culture. He made it plain that there was no work "beneath" him—even the work of a servant. For example, he willingly took on himself the menial job of washing feet. While it proved to be an ideal object lesson for the teacher to use, there seems little doubt that the way he used it, far from divorcing spiritual and secular, actually demonstrated to his disciples how even the most mundane and dirty of tasks can serve others and honor God.

Paul

Among New Testament writers, Paul has most to say about the role of work. As we'll see in the next chapter, in 1 Corinthians Paul teaches that we should work out our calling in whatever context we find ourselves. This is important for our current age where "full-time Christian service" is seen as the ultimate way of serving God—something more spiritual and satisfying than "secular work." Under this false value system, Christians will never find a strong sense of fulfillment and value in the tasks God has given them, because they will be forever dreaming of a "better" way to serve. Paul makes the same point in other letters. For example, in Colossians 3:23–24 he writes:

> Whatever you do, work at it with all your heart, as working for the Lord, not for human masters, since you know that you will receive an inheritance from the Lord as a reward. It is the Lord Christ you are serving.

N. T. Wright comments on these verses: "The task may appear unimportant or trivial, but the person doing it is never that, and he or she has the opportunity to turn the job into an act of worship."[1] What seems clear from Paul's teachings is that:

- *All work is of value and significance*, in spite of the status (or lack of it) given by the surrounding culture.

- *There is no hierarchy of tasks in God's economy.* As Eugene Peterson writes, "Any work done faithfully and well is difficult. It is no harder for me to do my job than for any other person, and no less. There are no easy tasks in the Christian way; there are only tasks which can be done faithfully or erratically, with joy or resentment."[2] Neither are there "spiritual" tasks and "secular" ones.

- *Everything we do needs to be connected with who we are in Christ.* This is reflected in Paul's view of his own work. He seemed not to regard his tentmaking trade as a means to an end, but as something that had real value in itself. About this Paul Stevens comments: "The New Testament treats work in the context of a larger framework: the call of God to live totally for him and his kingdom. Therefore Paul was not, strictly speaking, a bi-vocational missionary, but rather mono-vocational by integrating daily work with all aspects of his kingdom life."[3] This is reinforced in Paul's teaching as seen in Colossians 1:10, "As you learn more and more how God works, you will learn how to do *your* work" (*The Message*).

If the Bible gives us no reason to create a spiritual/secular distinction, then where did this split come from?

Monasticism

In the following chapter on calling, we'll look further at how the early church became influenced by the surrounding Greek/ Roman culture of its day. Despite the insistence of both Jesus and Paul that our faith infuse every part of our life, it took only a century or so after them for the church to adopt these dualistic ideas and view the spiritual and the physical as separate entities.

Biblical texts (such as Luke 10:38–42 where Jesus comments on Martha's criticism of Mary) came to be used to support a view that certain tasks were more spiritual than others. An ever-so-subtle twist in the message of this incident led to the "contemplative life" being seen as far better and more spiritual than the "active life." This dualistic view was quickly reinforced by the development of a "clergy" class and then the phenomenon of monasticism.

By the time Christianity became the official religion of the Roman Empire, the distinction between clergy and laity was clearly evident. With the insistence in the eleventh century on celibacy for the clergy, the demarcation between priesthood and laity was complete. The clergy inevitably acquired an aura of spiritual power, status, and privilege. Ordinary people were relegated to second-class status. The spiritual/secular chasm had opened wide.

Monasticism, somewhat unintentionally, reinforced this growing worldview. The movement to set up institutions dedicated to fostering the spiritual life arose in part because of the nominalism of the church. In the Christianized Roman Empire, believers were no longer a minority. In that atmosphere, discipleship quickly became diluted. When everyone is a "Christian" in name and faith is assumed, then faith loses its sharpness.

With the best of intentions, reformers tried to separate themselves from this "cultural" Christianity and to strive for spiritual growth in communities that were distinct from the world around them. So the notion arose that those who wanted to direct their thoughts uninterrupted toward God must not be distracted by the activities of a profession or by family concerns. (In fact, while manual work was not totally despised in monasteries, it was definitely secondary to "more important tasks.")

Luther and Calvin

It wasn't until the Protestant Reformation that this dualism was effectively challenged. Martin Luther had been a monk, but as he studied the New Testament his theology was turned on its head. His growing conviction about justification by faith soon led him to embrace a belief in the priesthood of all believers. Monks and clergy, Luther realized, were no more valued in God's economy than anyone else. In fact, all believers have a "priestly calling" in whatever roles they undertake.

Though different from Luther on a number of counts, John Calvin also promoted the belief that all work is "spiritual" in character. He emphasized the transformational nature of work and, with it, social action. Calvin challenged all believers "to work, to perform, to develop, to progress, to change, to choose, to be active, and to overcome until the day of their death or the return of their Lord."[4]

Yet, in spite of the efforts of Luther and Calvin, the church has never really freed itself from the clergy/laity distinction. We can talk all we like about "the priesthood of all believers," but in reality our churches are a long way from this ideal. Tasks *are* divided into spiritual and secular, and roles *are* distinguished according to "spiritual value."

Nineteenth-Century Evangelism

Much of this has to do with a narrowing of our understanding of salvation. In the late nineteenth century, salvation came to be viewed in largely individualistic and spiritualized terms. Dwight Moody, the famous North American evangelist, was a good example of this tendency. He viewed his role as essentially to "save souls." In fact, he used to say, "I look upon this world as a wrecked vessel. God has given me a lifeboat and said to me, 'Moody, save all you can.'" If God's real concern is only to see souls saved, then those who preach, run crusades, go overseas on missionary service, and so forth become more important than others. For they are doing what is closest to God's heart, doing what will ultimately be the only important work eternally. In this sort of theological worldview, everyone else can best find significance by contributing financially to the "work of God," praying for "full-time workers," or developing a "ministry" of their own.

"Secular work" is valued only inasmuch as it contributes to the "evangelization" of the world. Employment is useful primarily because it gives us an opportunity to "witness" to our non-

Christian workmates, and to earn money in order either to do "ministry" or to support others in "ministry." Acts of service and mercy are essentially viewed as a means to an end. By doing these things, we hope to attract people to Christianity and so "save their souls." Likewise, the value of friendship building with non-Christians is mainly that we can earn the right to share the "gospel" with them.

The "Full" Gospel Message

This contrasts sharply with a more holistic biblical mandate. As we've seen in chapter 3 on God's transforming work, God's intention is to put right the whole cosmos (see Col. 1, Rom. 8, Eph. 1, among other passages.) Remember Eugene Peterson's paraphrase of Colossians 1:20, which we also looked at in chapter 3:

> All the broken and dislocated pieces of the universe—people and things, animals and atoms—get properly fixed and fit together in vibrant harmonies, all because of his death, his blood that poured down from the cross. (*The Message*)

God's redeeming work involves the restoration of all four foundational relationships—with him, with ourselves, with one another, and with the rest of creation. To be sure, our relationship with God is absolutely central to this restoration, but it does not—indeed, cannot—stand in isolation from the other relationships. One automatically affects the others. Salvation involves *all* of these relationships.

We believe in the importance of evangelism. In fact, both of us have devoted much of our lives to spreading the good news. However, we don't believe in an evangelism that is disconnected from making disciples, or in a relationship with God that is disconnected from all other relationships. True evangelism leads believers to live as the servants of God in the *whole* of life, including our daily work.

CLOSING THE GAP

If we are to see the true significance of all the work we do, then we simply must deal with the dualism that dominates our view of the Christian life. It's not biblical, and so it is counterproductive to our aim of seeing God at work in this world of his. It is only as we learn to work *with* God, to see that what we do is connected with what God is doing, that we will close the false gap between secular and spiritual. A prayer of Richard Foster's echoes the desire to discover this kind of integration:

> *The day has been breathless, Lord. I stop now for a few moments and I wonder:*
>
> *Is the signature of the holy over the rush of the day? Or have I bolted ahead, anxiously trying to solve problems that do not belong to me?*
>
> *Holy Spirit of God, please show me:*
>
> *How to work relaxed*
> *How to make each task an offering of faith*
> *How to view interruptions as doors to service*
> *How to see each person as my teacher in things eternal;*
> *In the name of him who always worked unhurried. Amen.*[5]

ⅠⅠⅠⅠⅠⅠⅠⅠⅠⅠⅠⅠⅠⅠⅠⅠⅠⅠⅠⅠⅠⅠⅠⅠⅠⅠⅠⅠⅠⅠⅠⅠⅠⅠⅠⅠUP CLOSE & PERSONAL

1. Have you heard anyone talk in tones similar to the piece at the start of this chapter? How prevalent do you think this kind of thinking is in your church context?

2. Read Luke 10: 38–42. Discuss what you think Jesus is explicitly and implicitly saying about Mary's and Martha's activities. Why do you think we assume that Jesus' commentary on their different tasks was an either/or rather than a both/

and? (That is, his rebuke of Martha was a not comment about the value of her housework, but about affirming the validity of Mary's choice.)

3. Why do you think we have developed such a dualistic view of work? Try to identify ways in which it affects your own attitude toward the various tasks you do in the week.

EXERCISE

Refer back to the list of all the roles and tasks you fulfill during your week, which you compiled at the end of the introduction. Reflect on each of the tasks, asking yourself the following:

- How do I feel about the *value* of this task?

- What in this role do I find fulfilling and significant? Why? What do I find mundane, boring, pointless, and insignificant? Why?

- How much do I feel I am serving Christ when I do this work?

- What about the tasks and roles I feel negatively toward? Do I think this is primarily because they don't fit in well with my unique mix of giftings and temperament, or because I have not been able to connect what I do with what God is doing?

SUGGESTION FOR A GROUP ACTIVITY

Have members prepare the above questions beforehand (or in a time of personal reflection at the beginning of the group meeting). Then, either in pairs or in the whole group, invite members to share their discoveries about themselves.

WORKING WITH GOD

8

WORK AS CALLING

An Invitation to Vocation

Because of our involvement with numerous Christian organizations and churches, we both have had occasion over the years to see their application forms—the detailed set of questions they hand to anyone who is considering joining their staff as a "full-time Christian worker." Filling in these documents is surely a marathon activity. As you labor with all sorts of probing questions, you begin to wonder, "Am I really good enough for this position?" But no question is as difficult to pin down as the one that—in one form or another—asks: "What *call* do you feel to this work?"

THE CHRISTIAN CALL

The "call" has certainly become part of the language of evangelicals. We hear it used in a number of different ways. "I feel called to the ministry." "My work is my calling." "I sense the call of God on my life." "God has called me to Africa." You don't have to be in the church too long to realize that if you aspire to leadership, you'd better be prepared to explain what direct communication you've had from God. In some more legalistic circles, this may even involve a request for specific Bible verses, prophetic words, or incidents that "prove" God has spoken to you.

The older word *vocation* used to have the same meaning. It comes from the Latin *vocatio*, a calling. In modern use, it usually refers to a person's career or profession. For example, "I'm thinking of taking up law as a vocation." However, it is still used sometimes (especially in Catholic circles) to mean God's call to a particular Christian role.

BIBLICAL PERSPECTIVES ON "CALLING"

The idea of vocation or calling is very much present in the Bible, but in a surprisingly different way. There it doesn't so much concern *what we do* but *who we belong to*. Biblical calling is not about tasks; it is about our identity. Or, to put it another way, a calling is to join someone—not to do something or go somewhere. Neither is it exclusive. It's not limited to pastors and ministers, cross-cultural missionaries and "full-time Christian workers."

Here's the startling point. *All* of us are called. And what is it that we're called to? The biblical answer: To be followers of Jesus, his disciples. Any roles we play or tasks we do are simply out-workings of our call to follow him.

CALLED TO BELONG, BE, AND DO

First and foremost, we are called to belong. In the Scriptures, the word *calling* carries a sense of intimacy. God calls each of us by name, and he invites us to belong to him. For example, God states through his prophet Hosea in 11:1, "When Israel was a child, I loved him, and out of Egypt I called my son." Here is a call to relationship with God, and with it, to be a part of his family. Matthew writes about Jesus: "Going on from there, he saw two other brothers, James son of Zebedee and his brother John. . . . Jesus called them, and immediately they left the boat and their father and followed him" (Matt. 4:21–22).

We are not called *out of* the world. We find our true identity as God's people *in* the world that God made. This is expressed through living a life of transformation and of service:

> You, my brothers and sisters, were called to be free. But do not use your freedom to indulge the flesh; rather, serve one another humbly in love. (Gal. 5:13)

> Let the peace of Christ rule in your hearts, since as members of one body you were called to peace. (Col. 3:15)

> For God did not call us to be impure, but to live a holy life. (1 Thess. 4:7)

> I urge you to live a life worthy of the calling you have received. (Eph. 4:1)

> But you are a chosen people, a royal priesthood, a holy nation, God's special possession, that you may declare the praises of him who called you out of darkness into his wonderful light. (1 Pet. 2:9–10)

Os Guinness puts it this way:

> Calling means that our lives are so lived as a summons of Christ that the expression of our personalities and the exercise of our spiritual gifts and natural talents are given direction and power precisely because they are not done for themselves, or for our families, or our businesses or even humankind, but for the Lord, who will hold us accountable for them.[1]

So our calling or "vocation" is to belong to God. The daily work we do is an expression of our calling, *but it is not that calling*. However "spiritual" it may appear, our daily activity is not (biblically speaking) our "vocation" or our calling. It is simply the way we work out that calling, the way we express our love of God, the way we put into practice our service for him. Whether we clean floors or preach sermons is, in God's eyes, not the issue. Whatever our work may be, his concern is how faithfully we live his way.

SO HOW DID WE DEVELOP SUCH A "WARPED" VIEW OF CALLING?

The seeds of a corrupted view of calling were sown, as we noted in the previous chapter, early on in the history of the church, which became heavily influenced by the dualism of the surrounding Greco-Roman culture. Soon, only priests, monks, and nuns were considered to have a "religious" vocation. They were called to the "contemplative life" of prayer—set apart from the active life of ordinary, everyday work. Even Augustine—who praised the work of farmers, merchants, and tradespeople— distinguished between the "active life" and the "contemplative life." At times, it might be necessary to follow the active life but, according to Augustine, one should choose the other wherever possible. This type of thinking encouraged both monasticism and professional church leadership. People were supposed to be "called" to these more "spiritual" roles. In other words, "calling" or "vocation" became almost exclusively defined by the roles of the clergy and religious orders.

When Martin Luther began teaching that all Christians are called and that daily work is part of our calling, his ideas were revolutionary. Monasticism, Luther said, was not a unique class or special order. The work of monks and nuns was no higher in God's eyes than the normal work, performed in sincere faith, of a farmer or homemaker. John Calvin further developed this idea of daily work as Christian calling. It wasn't long, however, before particular jobs became specially identified as Christian vocations. Soon, the concept that our calling is primarily about belonging to Jesus began to drift into the background.

Consequently, while "calling" was once too narrowly defined, it now became so closely identified with particular occupations that the words *vocation, calling,* and *profession* simply became synonyms for *job.* While this emphasis began with the Puritans, it was mainly due to the influence of the Enlightenment and the Industrial Revolution that "vocation" became identified with occupation or career with no real spiritual connections. It is hardly surprising, then, that many people today speak of their vocation without any reference to a Christian calling. The wider culture has "wrestled" the word *vocation* off the Puritans and emptied it of its Christian meaning.

In spite of Luther's efforts, the church has never really freed itself from the clergy/laity distinction, and the two-tiered value system of the medieval church has largely remained in place. In church circles, a "real" calling is still thought to be one that involves a person in pastoral leadership or cross-cultural mission work. And because of our emphasis on being called to "do," invariably a calling is seen as something that takes us out of our current situation as God "leads" us into a new one.

WORKING OUT OUR CALLING WHEREVER WE ARE

It's exactly this type of mentality that Paul spoke about in his first letter to the Corinthians. Certain people within the church had been teaching that it was more spiritual for them to be single, with the implication that if married people really wanted to grow spiritually, then they should leave their partner.

Paul took pains to dismiss this idea. In 1 Corinthians 7, he argues that we should not think that God's call on our lives requires us to change our circumstances (that is, relationships, location, social position, employment, and so forth). On the contrary, the norm should be that we remain where we are and allow God to transform us, our relationships, our tasks, and our whole perspectives within that context. Paul is perfectly clear on the subject: "Each person should remain in the situation they were in when God called them" (1 Cor. 7:20). About this passage Gordon Fee says:

> The call to Christ has created such a change in one's essential relationship (with God) that one does not need to change in other relationships (with people). These latter are transformed and given new meaning by the former. Thus one is no better off in one condition than in the other.[2]

Paul was not advocating that we should never change our circumstances—simply that the call to follow Jesus means we can serve Christ *wherever we are*. Our context for serving may indeed change, but rather than *seeking* change in our situation, we should be working to discover ways that our calling to follow Jesus can be lived out through our current circumstances.

CONCLUSION

Have you received a call? You certainly have, if you've set out to follow Jesus. For his call to you is a call to be in relationship with him and to be part of the family of God. Your vocation is to work with him in order to transform your whole life. As you do this, you will increasingly find yourself able to serve him even further—by helping transform whatever part of the world you find yourself in.

‖‖‖‖‖‖‖‖‖‖‖‖‖‖‖‖‖‖‖‖‖‖‖‖‖‖‖‖‖‖‖‖‖‖UP CLOSE & PERSONAL

1. Have you ever had to justify yourself or provide "evidence" for being called to a particular role? If so, what happened?

2. How do you feel about your current tasks? To what extent does your church community affirm and support you in these tasks?

3. Have you ever considered changing jobs or location? On what basis do you think people should consider changing jobs? Are there times when their reason might not be valid? If so, what particular reasons would you consider invalid for changing jobs?

4. Discuss Gordon Fee's statement, "The call to Christ has created such a change in one's essential relationship (with God) that one does not need to change in other relationships (with people). These latter are transformed and given new meaning by the former. Thus one is no better off in one condition than in the other."

EXERCISE

Refer back to your list of roles/tasks at the end of the introduction. Spend some time pondering how each one fits into your calling to follow and serve Jesus. Then use the following outline to write a statement of calling for yourself.

Jesus Christ has called me [*your name*] to belong to and follow him. This calling is presently expressed in being committed to [*your church community*], and specifically to [*Christian family/ friends/mission or other groups you belong to*], as well as serving in the following roles and tasks: [*List your specific roles and tasks, such as husband/wife, father/mother, son/ daughter, friend; employee/employer/profession/paid employment; unpaid/voluntary roles; roles in church community and neighborhood*].

Feel free to personalize your statement. For example:

Jesus Christ has called me, John Smith, to belong to, know, and follow him.

This calling is presently expressed outwardly through being a member of Harrisville Christian Fellowship, and particularly by being committed to Jeremy Ronaldson, Frank and Margaret Jones, Mark McCutcheon, and Mary and Jerry Cruz. My calling is also expressed through the following roles, tasks, and relationships:

- Husband to Marilyn
- Father to Samuel and Whitney
- Engineer with the Harrisville City Council
- Board member of Redwood Park School Board of Trustees
- Coach of the Harrisville boys' Under 10 rugby team
- Friend to Bob, Jack, Tom F., Steve, Paul, and Richard
- Neighbor to Kelvin and Sandra, Mrs. Grantham, Jenny and George
- Member of the church pastoral care team
- Helper at the Harrisville Refugee Centre

The listed roles are the main (but not the only) outward expressions of my calling to follow Jesus. As his co-worker, I will endeavor to use all opportunities to serve him and to build his kingdom. I also recognize that the roles, tasks, and relationships I presently use to follow Jesus may well change as he directs and guides me.

9

WORK AS WORSHIP

Serving Our Ultimate Boss

As we've talked with numerous people over the years, it seems to us that, broadly speaking, there are three main ways Christians think about their work:

WORK AS A MEANS TO AN END: "I WORK TO LIVE"

The most common attitude (particularly to paid work) is one that views it as a means to an end. We work *in order to* live. It sees the purpose of our work simply as providing for our needs. This approach betrays a low view of work, and it's often fed by the dualism we have talked about in previous chapters.

For many people, they view at least some of their work as futile or meaningless, often expressed in such statements as:

- "I can't wait for the weekend."

- "When I earn enough cash, I'm out of here."

- "That darned lawn needs mowing again! I'm always having to do stuff around the house."

- "I do this job because it gives me the money to really live."

- "I work at the bank, but it's just a means to an end. What I really love to do is serve God by being involved in the church band, or by doing street evangelism, or whatever."

A number of years ago, Alistair conducted an extensive survey of Christians and their attitude toward work (see the epilogue for the context of this survey). One of the questions he asked was, "What is it that you struggle with most as a Christian in your work?" The results were startling. Many responded by noting that it wasn't the challenging work environment or culture, or that they were asked to do things that compromised their faith, but rather that they were deeply embarrassed and often annoyed by the behavior of other Christians in their place of employment.

The source of such difficulty was varied. For some, it was the "super-spiritual" and often insensitive utterances and behavior of excessively zealous believers, who seemed to take their faith seriously but not their work. For others, it revolved around the "sub-Christian" behavior of some who publicly identified themselves as believers. Still others noted the poor ethics of certain "Christian" firms that had a reputation within their industry for not paying bills on time, treating their employees poorly, or indulging in dubious competitive practices.

Alistair was also surprised by the number of Christian employers who said they were wary of hiring Christians. Many felt that Christians expected to get preferential treatment and special exemptions from their Christian bosses, which would create tension with other staff. For others, the wariness revolved around the past experiences of some "Christian" employees being poor workers—those who did not seem to take seriously their responsibility to work hard and well for their bosses.

Now, why would so many Christians be perceived as behaving so poorly in their employment? The simple answer is that if you carry a low view of your work and its place in God's economy, then these kinds of behaviors will all too likely be the result. If our work is largely seen as a means to an end, then we'll miss the connections between what we're doing and what God is about. Our work will be separated from our worship. It will be trivialized and underrated. We'll fail to take seriously what it means to be faithful to both God and our employer (or employees). Such a low opinion of work ultimately leads to becoming "idle" in our work, at least insofar as realizing our potential to serve both God and others.

WORK AS ALL-CONSUMING: "I LIVE TO WORK"

A second and also common attitude toward work belongs to those who are so caught up in it that their lives revolve completely around what they do. They end up "living to work."

When our work becomes all-consuming, we have embraced too high a view of it. We make work an object of worship, an idol. We do this by giving our work more importance than it's due. We separate our work and achievements from what God is doing and wants to do—basically pretending that we can rearrange the universe by our own efforts. It's then that we become compulsive in our work.

Our culture has a word for this: *workaholism*. When we become addicted to our work, our identity and value become so closely intertwined with it that we can't separate them. We become defined by what we do and achieve. This is dangerous. Society causes us to define who we are by the work we do. Notice when you meet new people that the question they ask fairly early in the conversation is "What do you do?" Now at one level, this is a fairly innocent question, so we don't want to make more out of it than we should. However, when we contrast the importance our culture places on finding out what work a person does with that of many non-Western cultures, the results suggest a tendency toward our work and our identity being fused.

Alternatively, in traditional New Zealand Maori culture, identity is based more on people and place—who you are related to and where you come from. This is a consistent feature of most indigenous cultures. And when we spent time in the Philippines, we were intrigued by how infrequently the question of what we did came up in an introductory conversation. People there wanted to know about our families, which indicated the relative value the Filipino culture placed on family relationships rather than work.

It's important to note that allowing our work to become all-consuming is not the same as treating it seriously. Neither does it mean that we shouldn't work hard. Nor that we shouldn't be passionate about our work. A biblical view of work understands that it has dignity and value. And God has worthwhile work for all of us to do.

At its best, work *should* be energizing and deeply fulfilling. However, there's a difference between loving and working hard at what we do and being addicted to our work. Work is not meant to be the most important thing in our lives, nor should it be degraded. It shouldn't lead us to idolatry, but neither should it lead us to be idle!

WORK AS WORSHIP: "I WORK AS AN EXPRESSION OF MY WORSHIP OF CHRIST"

This balance is best found when our work becomes *an act of worship,* just as it did for Brother Lawrence of the Resurrection (1614–1691), author of *The Practice of the Presence of God.* For fifteen years, Brother Lawrence worked as a cook in the kitchen of his monastery, and when he became unable to continue in this role, he lived out the remainder of his life making sandals.

At first he was deeply frustrated with the apparent insignificance of his role. But Lawrence eventually developed a deep spirituality of the ordinary, viewing every menial task as an opportunity to perform "little acts of communion with God." He developed practices that enabled him to experience God's presence and use every task and conversation as an opportunity for service and worship. Lawrence wrote:

> The times of activity are not at all different from the hours of prayer . . . for I possess God as peacefully in the commotion of my kitchen, where often enough several people are asking me for different things at the same time, as I do when kneeling before the Blessed Sacrament.[1]

His attitude was: "We must never tire of doing little things for the love of God, who considers not the magnitude of the work, but the love."[2]

Brother Lawrence understood an important point: our work is supposed to be intimately connected with our worship. In fact, our work often seems meaningless because we fail to endeavor at finding ways to connect our work with God's work. But when undertaken in partnership with God and his work, our tasks find significance and they become an expression of our love for God. This means that we can worship God by working *with* him when we're:

- changing diapers
- renovating a kitchen
- repairing a car
- looking after our grandchildren
- studying for an exam
- helping a customer find the right material
- fixing a computer, and so on

In Colossians 3:23–24, Paul puts it well when he states:

Whatever you do, work at it with all your heart, as working for the Lord, not for human masters, since you know that you will receive an inheritance from the Lord as a reward. It is the Lord Christ you are serving.

"*Whatever* you do." Work can—and should—be an act of worship. If we identify worship as what happens only on Sunday, it becomes a pale reflection of what God views as worship. For true worship is about the constant reorientation of our lives toward God and God's purposes for us. It's about offering all we are and all we do to God. In fact, the New Testament hardly ever uses the word *worship* to refer to what Christians do when they gather together.

Mostly, worship is used to talk about the way we are urged to offer the whole of our lives to God in his service. Think about, for example, Paul's words to the Romans: "Therefore . . . offer your bodies as a living sacrifice" (Rom. 12:1). This is a pivotal point in Paul's argument to the Romans. And he uses one of his favorite words, *therefore*. It's there to alert the hearer/reader that what Paul has said and what he is about to say are thoroughly linked. He's tying it all together: "Taking everything I've said up to now into account, here's what I want you to do; here is what it means for living and working."

Eugene Peterson captures this well in his paraphrase of Romans 12:1–2:

So here's what I want you to do, God helping you: Take your everyday, ordinary life—your sleeping, eating, going-to-work, and walking-around life—and place it before God as an offering. Embracing what God does for you is the best thing you can do for him. Don't become so well-adjusted to your culture that you fit into it without even thinking. Instead, fix your attention on God. You'll be changed from the inside out. (*The Message*)

1. This is an act of worship for the *home* and the *marketplace,* not just inside the church building. When Paul

so deliberately located worship in the physical business of living and working, he would have shocked some of his Greek hearers who tended to despise the material aspects of life, thinking that God (and spirituality) was concerned only with ethereal matters.

2. Paul disagrees. "Don't become so well-adjusted to your culture." In other translations, "not conforming to *the present age*" is used. It's a phrase Paul uses to contrast with "the age to come," where God's priorities and values rule. Paul urges us not to let the present age—our surrounding culture—dictate terms. We should not presume that how it expects us to think and be motivated, to work and relate, to live and behave, is necessarily what God wants for us.

3. In a sense we're called to be countercultural—which is not to say that absolutely everything will be different. Rather than automatically accepting that we should work (among other activities) like everyone else in our culture, we should ask ourselves if we're aiming to follow Jesus, and if we are, could this mean we might work differently? And if we are to work differently, what does that mean? For Paul, it is a changing "from the inside out." The Greek verb he uses is *metamorpho*. Notice the resemblance to our English word *metamorphosis*—the radical change from one form to another, such as the caterpillar turning into the beautiful butterfly. Paul suggests that this is what God wants to do in our lives and in our work.

4. However, our metamorphosis doesn't just happen by autopilot. It requires careful and disciplined thought. That's why most English translations use the phrase, "By the renewing of your minds." We need to apply ourselves

to the business of thinking Christianly about our work. Otherwise, our surrounding culture will simply "squeeze us into its mold" (Rom. 12:1, J. B. Phillips). As our whole thinking and belief systems are renewed, this results in tangible, visible changes in the way we live and work.

‖‖‖‖‖‖‖‖‖‖‖‖‖‖‖‖‖‖‖‖‖‖‖‖‖‖‖‖‖‖‖‖‖‖UP CLOSE & PERSONAL

1. Which tendency are you most vulnerable to? Worshipping work (workaholism) or treating it as a means to an end? Why?

2. In what ways do you think your faith community could do better at valuing *all* work, undertaken as an act of worship (not just certain tasks that seem more significant to God)?

3. In *A Public Faith: How Followers of Christ Should Serve the Common Good* (Brazos Press, 2011), theologian Miroslav Volf says, "With regard to our success in work, we pray not so much for God to miraculously bring about a desired result but to make us willing, capable, and effective instruments in God's hand—which is what we were created to be in the first place" (p. 27). Discuss this statement with regard to what kind of help we can expect God to provide us in our work.

4. What would help you remember that when you work this coming week you can do so as an act of worship, knowing that you are serving Jesus?

10

WORK AS MISSION

Laboring for the Kingdom

Alistair has been haunted for a number of years by a statement made by William Diehl, sales manager for Bethlehem Steel:

> In the almost thirty years of my professional career, my church has never once suggested that there be any type of accounting of my on-the-job ministry to others. My church has never once offered to improve those skills which could make me a better minister, nor has it ever asked if I needed any kind of support in what I was doing. There has never been an inquiry into the types of ethical decisions I must face, or whether I seek to communicate my faith to my co-workers. I have never been in a congregation where there was any type of public affirmation of a ministry in my career. In short, I must conclude that my church really doesn't have the least interest in whether or how I minister in my daily work.[1]

Does this sense of frustration and disappointment resonate with you? It certainly does with us. When we start to gain a vision for our work being a part of our calling and an expression of our worship, it's to be expected that we look to our faith community for support, encouragement, and resourcing so we can serve God well in our work. In fact, Diehl hints that he would dearly love to be related to in the same way his church relates to cross-cultural missionaries or pastors. His cry is to be recognized and supported as a marketplace missionary.

But we are aware that those two words don't quite seem to fit together, do they? Marketplace missionary. In fact, the phrase borders on the oxymoronic. For the idea that mission can take place in our places of paid or unpaid work is not something too many Christians would consider normal. Put more bluntly, it doesn't seem quite right that we would commission engineers or sales representatives as missionaries in their weekly employment.

WHY NOT?

Why is this the case? Partly, because mission has often been associated with the work a select few believers called "missionaries" do in exotic and remote places. Closer to home, if we *do* recognize the missionary role of believers in our own community, then it is generally limited to a few particular tasks, such as evangelism, church planting, or perhaps some social service ministries.

We don't dispute the need for evangelism in the marketplace. Without work expanding our circle of contact with non-Christians in a natural way, we might otherwise develop few significant relationships with unbelievers. Although, even when it comes to evangelism, we think that many Christians live with far too much fear and self-consciousness about what is required. One of the best evangelists Alistair knows is a Christian who struggles with all sorts of questions about his faith (and the fact that we would think of him as an evangelist would horrify him!). But his colleagues appreciate the questions he asks as a fellow searcher and the fact that he doesn't pretend to have it all together. His questions invite their participation without fear of being set upon. He has a gift for whetting people's appetite to know more. The best evangelists aren't pumped up. They are just themselves, admitting honestly how it is for them.

But is mission in the workplace only about evangelism? We don't believe so. After all, mission is really God's work of bringing about his kingdom in this world. It's the work of transformation we looked at in chapter 3, "God's Transforming Work." Everything that contributes to this is important. God's kingdom impacts every area of human life and endeavor. This includes evangelism, which is the center or heart of mission. Missiologist David Bosch puts it in perspective when he writes, "Evangelism is calling people to become followers of Jesus. It is enlisting people for mission—a mission as comprehensive as that of Jesus." Mission is therefore the wider concept, incorporating everything that God intends to transform in this world.

WE ARE ALL MISSIONARIES

Recently, a significant change has taken place in Christian understanding that recognizes mission as the task of the *whole* people of God, not just those traditionally labeled "missionaries." It sees that the *whole* church is called to live the *whole* gospel in the *whole* of life, in a way that will impact the *whole* world.

Mission literally means "sending." It refers to what God sends Christians into the world to be and to do. The "whole church" means that mission is a task for the data entry worker, mother, policy analyst, neighbor, lawyer, volunteer club member, and advertising executive. It's a task for *all* who follow Jesus.

The "whole gospel" means that mission involves much more than just getting people to follow Jesus, though that's certainly an important part of it. It has to do with God's vision for us and for the world—a vision for all of creation to be whole again, complete and perfect. It's the bringing about of *shalom*, complete harmony and wholeness. Between God and us. Between us and other people, particularly those we struggle to get along with. Between us and the rest of God's creation. And also living in peace within ourselves. In other words, the whole gamut of transformation we have talked about in previous chapters.

It is the picture of the fulfillment of this dream that we see in Revelation 21 as heaven meets earth and *shalom* is realized in the establishment of a redeemed city, the New Jerusalem. So even now, *our* work is an act of eager anticipation. We live according to the values of a community that is still to come. When Jesus told us not to be anxious about material concerns, but to seek first the kingdom (Matt. 6:25–34), he implied that our preoccupation is more important than our occupation. The way we go about our work is a reflection of what our hearts and minds are set on. It is a vision of the kingdom of heaven that directs and inspires our work.

We are invited to become part of the answer to the prayer that Jesus taught us to pray, "Your kingdom come, your will be done, on earth as it is in heaven" (Matt. 6:10). God invites us to personalize this challenge in our work so that this prayer becomes, "Your will be done, Lord, starting with me and starting right now." This may involve sharing our faith sometimes. It will definitely mean attempting to live with integrity. It will also involve creating and pursuing what is good and resisting what is bad, selfless service, healing and restoring relationships, stewarding creation, working for justice and exercising mercy, helping people to become all God created them to be, developing loving, caring and unified communities, and much more.

The "whole of life" means that mission is a task encompassing and transforming our homes and our neighborhoods, our organizations and relationships, our environment, our politics, and our everyday "sleeping, eating, going-to-work, and walking-around life" (Rom. 12:1, *The Message*). And it definitely includes our places of work, the industries and professions we labor in much of the week. The "whole world" means that mission is not just for those who labor across the oceans. It's definitely for those of us who labor down the street, in the city, on the farm, in the classroom, and in the kitchen. It is the whole church living the whole gospel in the whole of life impacting the whole world. This is mission.

GOD'S MISSION, OUR COMMISSION

If this seems like too big a commission for us, it is—which is why another profoundly important truth that needs recapturing is that mission doesn't start with what *we* do in the world. Mission begins with what *God* is doing in the world and the part we have to play in God's mission. To put it another way: it is not about what we do *for* God, but about what we do *with* God. We are invited to do what we can, but in response to God's initiative. For it is first and foremost *God's* mission. We are sent by God into our places of work, to be his agents.

This is why we like the word *commission*. If we break it down into two parts, we see that the "co" or "com" is a prefix for "with," "alongside," or "together." The word assumes that mission is done *with* someone and that someone is God (and in a lesser sense, with one another). Being "com-missioned" involves working alongside God in God's mission to the world. Another way of putting this is how Charles Ringma (professor emeritus of missions and evangelism at Regent College, Vancouver) defines mission as *joining* God in God's caring, sustaining, and transforming activity on earth.[2] Without this critical truth, we can easily try to do what only God can do—and that is impossible. We're on dangerous ground if we start with an exalted view of the significance of what we are doing and a diminished view of what God is doing. This makes our God out to be much too small—and us much too big.

One implication of viewing ourselves as involved in God's already existing mission is that we assume that God is already on the job in our places of work. We don't arrive at our offices, classrooms, workshops, or retail shops bringing God with us. God is already there—at work among our colleagues, customers, students, organizations, businesses, and industries. Our starting point is to look for where God is already working to bring transformation, and then seek to co-mission with God.

Eugene Peterson reminds us:

> As Christians do the jobs and tasks assigned to them in what the world calls work, we learn to pay attention to and practice what God is doing in love and justice, in helping and healing, in liberating and cheering. . . . The Bible insists on a perspective in which our effort is at the edge and God's work is at the center.[3]

THE CHALLENGE

We believe the future of the church will be determined by the extent to which it is able to mobilize and provide resources and support for all its members for mission all the time. What a tragedy that many Christians continue to think that what they do most of the time doesn't matter to God. This is an outrageous lie that sadly obstructs them from pursuing God's mission through their work.

However, we do not emphasize the importance of mission in the marketplace by exalting the significance of the marketplace in itself, the way our consumerist culture does. Rather, we see that whole-of-life discipleship must include the marketplace. Brian Walsh and Richard Middleton write:

> The problem isn't that the Christian community is lacking in doctors, farmers, business people and musicians. The problem is that there are so few Christian doctors, farmers, business people and

musicians. Most of us are Christians and something else; we do not engage in our daily tasks integrally as Christians. . . . Well-meaning Christians are merely adding faith to their vocation rather than letting faith transform their vocation.[4]

We think that's spot on. If we have a truncated view of Christian mission that becomes associated only with what we do in our spare time, then our faith is really just an optional extra leisure time pursuit, no longer integral to all that we do. Or it becomes associated only with those particular moments when we feel more directly involved in evangelism at work.

The truth is that getting involved in God's mission in the marketplace is potentially thrilling, on the edge, and challenging. We appreciate the way Steve Brinn expresses it:

Why shouldn't Christians be up to their ears in tough stuff—and aren't most of our reasons for shying away from it shallow or false? From the time I entered business, more than 22 years ago, Christ to me has been a model of engagement. Dangerous engagement in life, where there was high exposure with questionable people and complicated issues, entailing prospects for great conflict and trouble. Christ's invitation to be like him led me, in the business context, from safe harbors to open water.[5]

Are you up to the challenge? (In chapter 12, you can read about how Wayne has sought to work this out.)

‖‖‖‖‖‖‖‖‖‖‖‖‖‖‖‖‖‖‖‖‖‖‖‖‖‖‖‖‖‖‖‖‖‖‖‖UP CLOSE & PERSONAL

1. What has been your understanding of "mission" and why?

2. Think about your own place/s of work. Try to identify where and how you have seen God already at work. What indications might you look for that God is working?

3. Discuss the implications of viewing yourself as a marketplace missionary.

4. What do you find most challenging or hard about sharing your faith in your work context/s? Why?

5. Share your own perception of how your faith community/church understands your work. What would be most helpful to you in feeling that they support, encourage, and provide resources for you?

If you're studying this book in a group, you may like to finish this session by praying the following together.

PRAYER OF COMMISSION

We are your people, Lord, called to follow, serve, and love you.
We acknowledge afresh our dependence on you.
We want to be co-workers in your mission to this world.
Empower us by your Spirit we ask.
Give us vision to see what you want us to do.
Give us insight to see what you are already doing.
Give us humility to serve without complaint, in whatever tasks are before us.
Give us courage to testify to your goodness and faithfulness.
Give us patience and endurance in the race you have set before us.
Give us hope to believe that ultimately you will reign in all places and all hearts.
Transform us, we ask.
May your kingdom come, here on earth, as it is in heaven.
Amen.

WORKING IT OUT

11

Engaged Work

Devotion on the Job

Servants, do what you're told by your earthly masters. And don't just do the minimum that will get you by. Do your best. Work from the heart for your real Master, for God, confident that you'll get paid in full when you come into your inheritance. Keep in mind always that the ultimate Master you're serving is Christ. The sullen servant who does shoddy work will be held responsible. Being a follower of Jesus doesn't cover up bad work. (Col. 3:22–25, *The Message*)

It was 10:00 a.m. Monday, and Hugh was already feeling bored and unmotivated, his mind drifting to the events of the previous weekend. It had been downhill pretty much from the start of the day. The boss had made his customary entrance, slapping a wad of edited papers on Hugh's desk without so much as a nod. Hugh groaned. He knew from hard experience what that meant. The week before, he'd done his best to draft the policy recommendation, even though his motivation was about as low as the FTSE 100. Of course, Hugh was by now hardened and cynical about the waste of time many of his efforts were. It was not uncommon for the boss to (seemingly out of the blue) change his mind and state that such-and-such a document or letter was no longer needed.

Survival in this office environment was not easy, but over time Hugh had subconsciously developed a number of effective (though short-term) diversionary tactics to get his head out of the prospect of another mind-numbing day. Without a thought, he clicked onto the Internet to check out the weekend's sports results. Sweet relief! His football team, Manchester United, had won away from home. All was well with the world!

ARE YOU ENGAGED?

One of the big issues in the workforce today is worker engagement. Numerous surveys have been conducted in recent years that demonstrate a low level of motivation, sense of ownership, and commitment by a high number of people in their jobs. Engagement has to do with being energized with our work. It leads to giving our all to the tasks at hand.

On the contrary, disengaged workers are those who just go through the motions. They struggle to exhibit any strong sense of ownership and responsibility for their work. In fact, if bedrock honesty was tapped, the truth is that such people would prefer to be somewhere else—they are there only because they lack other options.

So what determines the level of engagement in our work? Leadership writer Patrick Lencioni suggests that the three main reasons for disengagement are anonymity (feeling unappreciated and invisible), irrelevance (feeling our work doesn't really count or isn't valued), and immeasurement (inability to measure tangible results).[1] When these are our dominant feelings, our work is likely to be a miserable experience.

WHY CHRISTIANS SHOULD BE ENGAGED WORKERS

Let's face it, all of us have elements of our jobs and roles we don't particularly enjoy, due perhaps to one of the reasons stated above. But it could be because we're not well suited to the tasks or we don't get along with our colleagues. While there is no doubt all these factors make it extra challenging to be engaged in our work, as Christians we don't have to be limited by them.

If we passively rely on our bosses and work environments to give us the feel-good factor, or if we spend much of our time wishing we had a better job, then we'll never take responsibility for our call to give 100 percent, to be truly engaged. We are, after all, working for the ultimate boss. Nothing we do is ever wasted. God values and treats as worthwhile *every* offering of work we produce—whether or not others around us appreciate or acknowledge our efforts. What's more, it's not necessarily *what* we do but *how* we do it that most counts.

Let us share several examples of how challenging (yet critical) it is to work this out in our daily lives. We hope these stories will both encourage and challenge you.

THE PRISON VOLUNTEER

Wayne is a volunteer with the chaplaincy service at our local prison, which he genuinely believes is worthwhile work. However, the way he is treated as a volunteer is often appalling. In spite of the written rhetoric, it is clear that management does not value the volunteers. In fact, the cynic might observe that the volunteers are just an irritant to them!

He is frequently mucked around—going to a lot of effort to see an inmate or lead a study—only to arrive and discover it is no longer convenient or possible. Sometimes he walks into a unit and is completely ignored by the staff. Other times, he is in the middle of a deep conversation or a tender moment in a study or service and an officer walks in to announce that they have to stop—right now—without a moment's consideration of what is being interrupted. He and his wife Jill were once ordered to immediately leave the prison grounds. No apology or acknowledgement of this wrong order has ever been given. What do these semi-regular experiences communicate to him? That to all intents and purposes, his work doesn't matter.

Some time ago, his volunteer status ran out and needed to be renewed. Although the prison has a system to alert volunteers to this biennial occurrence, that system failed. So one day he discovered he could not enter the gates. The Bible study and services he led, and the men he visited, were now left to their own devices. The trust relationships he had formed with the guys were now put on hold. It took six weeks for him to renew his status, and it could have taken much longer if it wasn't for an advocate within the system.

According to Lencioni's three signs of a miserable job, going into the prison should be a miserable experience for Wayne. He is completely anonymous to the management and most of the staff. It is clear that the system considers his contribution as largely irrelevant. And given the type of work he does, measuring whether he is making any real difference is inherently problematic.

In his worst moments, he finds himself angry, resentful, and feeling completely undervalued. And then he is reminded of *who* it is he is actually working for and *who* he is serving. It's as if God says to him, "Get over yourself, Wayne! Think about why you are really doing this. You don't need to be affirmed by the system. You know what you're doing is important to me. Treat each interaction, each visit, as an offering of worship."

In his best moments, he recognizes that the men he spends time with deserve his very best. And on the days when he questions the worth of his efforts, or is struck by how unsuited he is for some of what he does, he has to remind himself that none of this is an excuse for not giving his all.

Shoddy or careless work is not what God expects of him. And it cannot be excused because he feels undervalued, anonymous, or like he's working in a job that doesn't fit him. The words of Brother Lawrence keep ringing in his ears! (Read them again in chapter 9 if you can't remember!)

"CHRIST AS MY EMPLOYER"

The second story was told to Alistair by a friend, about someone who made a deep impression on him. Here's what he said
about the person concerned:

> He was one of the first Christians I had met who believed that he
> served Jesus Christ in the marketplace. He has done well in busi-
> ness and was part of middle management for his firm. Now his
> commitment was being tested. He felt enormous pressure because
> he had refused to do something immoral to keep a client. He also
> suspected that he would lose his job because he wouldn't go along
> to get along. He was right.
>
> A few weeks later he was told that the company was making some
> organizational changes and his services were no longer needed. He
> knew, and his boss knew, that the real reason was not the given
> reason for the dismissal. He was out of work for weeks, and when
> he found a new position it was for less pay.
>
> Yet he had gone through the experience with an unflinching faith
> and I was impressed. I told him as much when we were having one
> of our regular breakfasts together. He responded, "I serve Jesus
> Christ at my work. It's nice to get a check every month, but really
> I see Christ as my employer. He honors those who honor him."

MARKETPLACE PRIEST

> The third example comes from the son of lifelong missionaries.
>
> I have always felt the tension between the sacred and the secular. I
> felt this tension most when I was about to graduate from university
> with honors in finance and engineering, and I readied myself to
> enter the marketplace.
>
> Here I was, a follower of Jesus, feeling conflicted about using a first-
> rate education in the business world. "What's redeeming about a

job in the marketplace if the ultimate objective is only an increased stock price or a better profit margin?" I asked myself. "Would Jesus become a management consultant or investment banker?"

Over the years, I have come to realize that I was operating under a paradigm that segmented all earthly activities into two distinct categories—the sacred and the secular—and that these categories did not overlap. In this paradigm, working in the marketplace most certainly belonged to the latter category.

Some believers dissolve this tension between the sacred and the secular by simply becoming pastors or missionaries. I almost did just that. But there is another way to address this tension.

God gives each of us different gifts, passions and callings, and for some of us, these gifts are in the realm of business. If our calling is to advance God's kingdom through business, then that is our highest calling.

Whatever our calling from God—whether in the marketplace or in the church—our calling is noble and sacred, and the old paradigms fall away. In fact, the sacred and the secular overlap and coexist. Personally, I have found a greater integration of my work (the "secular") and faith (the "sacred") with the realization that I can minister in the marketplace through my business. All aspects of my life, including my work in business, are ministry when they further God's purposes.

I have also come to realize that doing business can be a spiritual activity that has redeeming and sacred value, thereby resolving that age-old tension within Christianity. We need not feel conflicted when we seek to serve God through our work. The marketplace is as legitimate a venue as any other for serving others to the glory of God, and doing so makes our very work a sacred act.

OTHER EXAMPLES

British communicator Mark Greene tells the story of a woman who worked as a receptionist. She decided to make a habit of letting the phone ring an extra two times before she answered it, so that during those two rings she could stop and ask God to help her be more attentive both to the person and also to God. Unsurprisingly, it changed her way of relating to customers, and her sense of being attentive to God.

Several years ago, Wayne visited York Minster, an ancient cathedral in England. The volunteer tour guide who showed him around was a retired gentleman who not only took great delight in explaining the history of the building, but also gently inquired about Wayne and what he was interested in. Early in the conversation he leaned over and asked softly, without a hint of judgment, "So tell me, are you a tourist or a pilgrim?"

A girlfriend of Alistair's, during his university days, used to write four capital letters at the top of each page of her notes: "AMDG." Alistair was mystified, so eventually he asked her what they stood for. She said that they represented the Latin words *Ad Majorem Dei Gloriam.* Translated into English they read, "For the greater glory of God." Here was a constant reminder of who this young woman was studying for.

IIIIIIIIIIIIIIIIIIIIIIIIIIIIIIIIIIIIIIIIIUP CLOSE & PERSONAL

1. Read Colossians 3:22–25 (listed at the beginning of this chapter). What kind of work would you consider "shoddy" in your employment?

2. Which of the stories/examples in this chapter resonates with you most? Why?

3. Brainstorm together some practices that might help you to remind yourself who you are ultimately working for.

EXERCISE

Think about your own work, paid or unpaid. On a scale of 1 to 10, what is your level of engagement? Then attempt to identify the factors contributing to this.

12

Confessions of a Car Dealer

Putting It All Together

WAYNE'S STORY

Some years ago I became involved, somewhat unexpectedly, in the business of buying and selling cars. This chapter tells my story, and the struggle to express my call to follow Jesus as a car dealer. I hope my honest reflections will help put some flesh and bones on the issues we have been grappling with.

Now let me say right from the start that I'm fully aware of the low esteem given to my "profession" (which is perhaps an overly generous term). We seem to have done particularly poorly on the "most trusted professions" annual survey, competing with Congressmen for the "least trusted" tag, according to recent Gallup polls.

I've also learned to live with the jokes, such as the one that asks when you can tell that a car dealer is lying (answer: whenever he moves his lips!). Given all this, you might fairly ask, how can anyone professing to follow Christ sell cars for a living? In fact, many people might consider the very phrase "Christian car dealer" to be somewhat oxymoronic.

Well, it certainly had its challenges. But I came to the conclusion early on that it's exactly industries like car dealing that God most wants (and needs) to transform. At any rate, I enjoyed and valued my time in business. While I no longer trade as a car dealer, I am grateful for what I learned and for the tremendous opportunities it gave me to work with God. It was a great ride (no pun intended).

HOW IT ALL BEGAN

For much of my adult life, I worked for Christian organizations. While financial insecurity was often a reality, my wife and I were aided by the generous support of family and friends. After a few years, however, things began to change. It is said that necessity is the mother of invention, and when our organization (Signpost Communications) faced an uncertain future because of financial sustainability, we were forced to look for small business opportunities. To be blunt, we realized that for the organization to survive, we had to find some way of paying the bills.

Although buying and selling cars was not something I naturally gravitated toward, a series of events led to a colleague and me importing secondhand vehicles from Japan. That it would mean eventually becoming a licensed car dealer never even occurred to me. If it had, then I would have felt the irony immediately and backed off.

This is because my one and only experience with a car dealer was negative. When I was young, I spied a freshly painted 1972 Holden (GM) Kingswood in a local dealer's yard. Mid-blue in color, it looked the part. For the first and last time in my life, I purchased a vehicle from a car dealer. Things were fine for the first six weeks, and then it happened: the paint began to bubble in various places. Soon vibrant shades of rust brown appeared across the body, showing evidence that the panel shop job had been substandard.

While there was little I could do about it, it did reinforce my growing stereotype of used car dealers. Back then, I resolved never to buy a vehicle from any of them again. In fact, that one and only experience of sales-yard antics convinced me that used car salesmen were about as useful to the economy as the polar icecap. And yet, here I was, unexpectedly a member of this despised profession!

THE LIFE OF A CAR DEALER

Dealing ethically with people in a highly unredeemed industry was one of a number of issues that soon confronted me. Another was what value I should place on the 20 to 25 hours per week I spent running the business. Initially, I confess, I viewed it as a means to an end. My heart was in Signpost Communications, but in order for us to survive we had to earn money. Deep down I knew it was inadequate to simply view the business as a place to earn a buck and a preaching opportunity. To be sure, mentally I ascribed to the view that God was interested in all work. But the reality was less clear-cut. At first I didn't find it all that easy to make a connection between my efforts at "God's work" and my activities as a car dealer.

Part of my dilemma was that I viewed the car industry as one of the key markets fueling our consumerism. I knew that millions of dollars were wasted every year on our fetish of driving the latest and greatest fashion. So was it even appropriate that I, a Christian, committed to living an alternative to the great Western dream, should get involved in an industry that furthered our consumerist tendencies?

But then I decided that despite the negative way cars were used and viewed, people still needed transport. While our wants may get tied up with our genuine needs, I was still serving people by providing them with good-quality, well-priced vehicles that they needed for getting themselves from place to place. Some of my toughest dilemmas revolved around how to serve clients who were quite willing to waste thousands of dollars more on a car than they needed to, or who seemed completely unconcerned about the environmental impact of their gas-guzzling SUV! I had to learn not to force my own convictions on them, but rather to find gentle and subtle ways of bringing influence. Short of withdrawing completely from society, there was no way we could divorce ourselves from the systems and structures of our communities.

I came to the conclusion that all industries need Christians, and it was our role to discover ways of redeeming and transforming those industries—of finding how we might work "Christianly" in them—especially in industries like selling secondhand vehicles, where customers desperately need people they can trust.

The primary question I asked myself through those years of car dealing was, "How can I do business Christianly?" Or to put it in another (and perhaps less clumsy) way, "How can I as a car dealer follow Jesus faithfully?" It seemed to me that doing this would involve much more than being honest, sharing my faith, and giving generously to "Christian causes."[1] It is not that these issues were unimportant or in any way peripheral. They were, however, insufficient in themselves.

In fact, I soon came to believe that my business should, over time, lead to a *distinctive* way of operating, one radically different from the norm.[2] This revolved around issues such as the way I bought and sold cars, how I priced them, the type of cars I sold, and how I related to customers, service providers, and other car dealers. Many of the ethical issues I confronted had wider social, economic, and environmental considerations, and there were tough issues and tensions to grapple with. All this meant that trying to run a car business with real integrity, and see it as genuinely contributing to God's work, became a fascinating journey of discovery.

SERVING OTHERS

Selling cars is essentially a service industry, but was it even possible to serve people altruistically and still make money from the business? The answer, I discovered, was a qualified yes. When dealing with people, I learned to carry uppermost in my mind the question, "Do I genuinely want the best for this person, or do I simply see them as an opportunity to make a sale?" I would love to be able to say categorically that my responses were always 100 percent for the good of the person, but that would be lying! However, I did grow in this area and certainly felt relaxed about serving people at the cost of losing a sale.

How did I serve people, then, through my business? For those wanting to buy a vehicle, I did so by:

- Helping them work out what they needed (this was often a long process, but absolutely critical if customers were to make a good choice).

- Giving them options to explore and suggesting they consider a car more suitable for their needs.

- Selling them a vehicle for a price that was hard to beat.

- Ensuring they knew they could come back to me if there was a problem.

- Being happy to provide ideas and options without making them feel they were obliged to buy from me.

I learned that some widely accepted practices actually worked against serving people well. For example, one was the kind of negotiation tactics generally employed by car yards. I call it the bargaining game. The problem with making a sale this way is that it generally undermined trust in the relationship and played with people's heads. Plus, it tended to favor those who knew the game and were able to play it well. It was both counter-productive and unfair. For these reasons, I abandoned the practice early in my business, replacing it with a set price structure.

Another industry practice was the strong encouragement for customers to finance their vehicles. I quickly discovered that there was a huge financial incentive for dealers to do this, as the commissions and kickbacks from the finance companies were a significant money earner for them. The result was that many people ended up buying vehicles they could not really afford, leaving them to struggle with high interest loans on a fast-depreciating asset. My contrasting approach was to do no finance deals and strongly encourage people to buy within their means. If customers felt they *had* to get finance, then my advice was to go to their bank. If they were not prepared to lend them the money, then they definitely couldn't afford it!

In order to serve people well, I sometimes gave advice that worked against making a sale. For example, I regularly told people to hold onto a good vehicle for a length of time in order to get the value out of it. Regular changing of vehicles almost invariably makes bad economics, because it will cost you each time you change. I knew this advice was potentially bad for my business, and there were some customers who chose not to change cars because of the advice I gave them! But I had to remind myself: Did I want to *serve* people or take advantage of them?

I also attempted to serve my business associates—the mechanics, custom agents, car groomers, and panel shops whose services I used. I did this by:

- Working hard to make my interactions and dealings with them enjoyable and fun experiences, as well as taking a genuine interest in them.

- Looking for ways we could make doing business with each other a win/win situation and recommending them to others.

- Being transparent and honest in my dealings, striving for integrity.

- Finding ways to help them out; for example, by offering to pay my account early where cash flow was difficult for a service provider, or by offering a vehicle where they needed transport for an emergency, and so on.

- Not expecting more of them than what was reasonable.

- Appreciating their work—and letting them *know* that I appreciated it.

BUILDING RELATIONSHIPS

Being in business was a great way to grow relationships—not just with clients, but also within the industry. I immensely enjoyed working with people who were part of the car scene. This resulted in opportunities to build friendships with my service providers and with other dealers. It was remarkable how often someone would open up to me about their struggles or ask me about faith issues. I put this down to taking time to be genuinely interested in them—creating the environment for trust to grow.

I also built a strong relationship with my Japanese agent, which was tremendously enriching. In fact, we became friends first and business associates second. My occasional trips to Japan were wonderful opportunities to spend time with this man, his workers, and his family. We had intriguing conversations in the car on the way to the auctions and while sitting in restaurants, listening to what was important to each other. At times he questioned me about my Christian beliefs, and why I lived the way I did. This enriching friendship would not have been possible without the business, which provided the context for the relationship.

DEVELOPING GIFTS

Being in business also resulted in a great deal of personal development, forcing me into situations where the reservoir of my potential was tapped in unexpected ways. My car sales work prompted responses from me never needed in other roles in my life. I found that latent within each of us are countless gifts and abilities that God delights in developing. His creativeness knows no limit.

For example, my business provided many opportunities to think laterally and come up with imaginative solutions. I never felt these were natural strengths of mine, but through the demands of my business God often helped me solve problems creatively. Someone might ring up in a panic because his vehicle had given up the ghost, prompting me to find a way to fill his immediate need so he could get by until a long-term solution was found. Or it might be through offering a customer another way of thinking about her requirements. The possibilities were endless, and I learned to delight in little bits of inspiration that came to me at just the right time. I viewed these as "acts of grace," which helped me to see how I could work in partnership with God. Of course, many of these growing skills were transferrable, so since God developed me in the business, I have been able to exercise those same abilities in other roles I now fulfill.

One outlet I found for expressing my values as well as my gifts was writing regular newsletters to all my past clients. I was able to provide information on the market, and on some relevant issue such as the true costs of running a vehicle, depreciation, financing, how to get the best value from your car, and so on. People appreciated this service, and many commented on how it gave them food for thought.

MORE THAN A CAR DEALER!

I am grateful for my years of car dealing. And I certainly have no doubt that this work counted, that it had real value in God's economy. However, the car business was only one of many roles I carried during the course of my week. I continued to work part time for Signpost Communications, and there were numerous unpaid tasks to do. They included being:

- A husband to my wife, Jill
- A father to our daughters—Maria, Kellie, and Melody— and occasional foster children
- Chairperson of the local school board of trustees
- Neighbor
- Home group member
- Youth group leader
- Friend
- Church member
- Homeowner

Collectively, I viewed all these roles as the expression of my call (or vocation) to follow Jesus. And I considered them all part of my work.

Of course, since those days, many of my roles have changed. It has taken a few years, but I now find myself thinking much more holistically about my days and weeks. All facets of my work mesh together as part of my vocation of following Jesus, and the paid/unpaid distinction now means little to me. Where the money to live on comes from is somewhat secondary to the value of the various tasks I feel called to fulfill. It's not that money is unimportant (we all have to live). Rather, it's that the value of work is never determined simply by whether or how much I get paid for it.

Nor does the enjoyment I find in the task dictate whether or not I see it as "work." I've come to accept that in every task there will be elements I enjoy greatly and others I find difficult, monotonous, and uninspiring. If I did only the things I enjoy, then there would be a lot left undone! Learning about my motivations, gifts, and temperament over the years has helped me make strategic choices about where to put my time and energy. But ultimately, I've learned the importance of putting at least some effort into tasks in which I'm *not* naturally gifted or motivated. God has much to teach me, and each activity has its place in the scheme of things, contributing to my service.

This has forced me to think long and hard about how even the most mundane tasks are connected to God's work in this world. Because I like order, I rarely lack the motivation to wash the dishes and mow the lawn. But it has taken time for me to understand how doing such work can serve others, express care for creation, and be an opportunity for me to learn discipline. Recognizing this has helped me take delight in doing these simple, menial chores well.

AN INTEGRATED VIEW

I'm fortunate. The nature of my paid work over the years has given me a certain amount of freedom, allowing me to be flexible in the way I use my time. Not everyone is blessed with such flexibility. I think all of us can learn, however, to be more integrated in the way we view time and our various roles. We can do this primarily by rejecting the paid/unpaid distinction as the main grid through which we value different tasks. Instead, we can learn to recognize how much the task allows us to reflect and further the kingdom of God.

For example, the raising of children is a strategic task. At no other stage of life have I had the opportunity to shape lives more than in those child-rearing years. I look back on them as the most important challenge of my discipleship. When I first began to appreciate the strategic role of parenting "work," my view of it changed dramatically.

Don't get me wrong, I still find some roles (and parenting was one of them) more difficult than others. Because of my temperament and gifting, I easily gravitate to those tasks that have a tangible and clear outcome. My utilitarian streak is still likely to complain at using "valuable" time to do something whose benefits are not immediately obvious. "It's not productive enough. I should be spending my time on things that produce *real* results!" But I have learned to allow my value system to be reshaped and to view all effort directed toward God as work.

This includes relationships. In fact, it *especially* includes relationships, for people are at the center of our calling to follow Jesus. People are the heart and soul of all work. Relationships do not (contrary to popular opinion) just happen. They are generally the result of working at them in a focused way.

So I am learning to be more flexible with my schedule and to hold my activistic goals a little more lightly. Frequently, God will bring across my path people who need my time. These are unique opportunities to serve, encourage, laugh with, cry with, and open up to others. My journey of faith requires me to give priority and attention to the small things that God is doing in the lives of the people I meet. Listening to them and responding in friendship and love will not come if I am always focused on the "tasks" I have set for myself. In fact, this process of realigning my priorities is still going on!

‖‖‖‖‖‖‖‖‖‖‖‖‖‖‖‖‖‖‖‖‖‖‖‖‖‖‖‖‖‖‖‖‖‖UP CLOSE & PERSONAL

1. If a used car salesman thinks he can work with God, anyone can! What comes out of Wayne's story that you can identify with? What other observations and solutions can you add?

2. Try engaging in the same exercise yourself. Put down on paper ways in which you have come to see your work as connecting with God's work. Now try to describe this to the group and invite them to quiz you further. Then offer to do the same for them.

3. What do you see as the greatest benefits that might come from realigning time to make relationships the priority? What are possible snags?

13

WORKING WORDS

Changing Our Terminology

We all know how important words are. They communicate more than just actions and ideas. Many words encapsulate and reinforce worldviews, ways of thinking. For this reason, we believe we simply must change our vocabulary when it comes to the issues this book raises. We are not talking just semantics. For the way words—such as *work*, *secular*, *calling*, and *ministry*—are used has so twisted the original intention that every time we use them, they are immediately heard, understood, and interpreted through the grid of the powerful worldview we have been seeking to challenge. Unless we change our vocabulary, we risk tripping up ourselves and others. Every time we use those words and expressions, we'll find ourselves reinforcing the old ways of thinking. Let's consider some specific words.

WORK

Because the word *work* has such a wide range of connotations, how can we make clear what we mean? Simply by using a more specific word. It's with paid work that most of the problems arise. So if that's what we're referring to, then *job*, *paid work*, or *employment* (or even the older word *occupation*) are options to consider using. If it's voluntary work or tasks around the home, then the words *task* and *role* become helpful. For example, "I've been working in my role as a school trustee." Or, "I've got a number of tasks to do around the house on Saturday. I think I'll be working all day at them."

FULL-TIME CHRISTIAN SERVICE

What do we mean when we say "full-time Christian service"? Generally, we're indicating people who invest most of their week in a role within a Christian organization or church. All of us are full time in Christian service, so to make the differentiation it's much better to say "church work," "paid church staff," "employed by a Christian (or mission) organization," "cross-cultural missionary," and so on.

SECULAR

Here's one word we think we should make every effort to ban from our vocabulary, unless we are referring to it in the negative sense (such as *secularization*). The images it conjures up almost entirely support a dualistic view of life. Remember, nothing in life is removed from God's sphere—only what we deliberately divorce. The process of secularization is a real trend, but it's not one that should include us. For in reality, all of life is meant to be connected with God and his work. Consequently, when we use the word *secular* we make an unbiblical and unhelpful distinction. Of course, it can be useful to talk about our involvement in different spheres of life. But the words we use to describe them need to be chosen more carefully.

Four helpful terms to distinguish these spheres are "marketplace," "community," "church," and "family." God is involved in all these arenas. When we exclude him, we are contributing to secularization. Sadly, Christians have virtually given in to this process in the marketplace and the community. We're not suggesting that the boundaries between these spheres of involvement are distinct. They're quite loose and overlap at many points. Most of us work in all four of them, but to varying degrees. Some of us invest most of our effort in the marketplace—the worlds of business, law, education, and industry. Others are able to give a majority of their energy and time to the family, community, or church. Consequently, rather than "the workplace" being interpreted as "the place of paid employment" or being limited to the marketplace, it really should refer to all of these spheres.

MINISTRY

Few words are more problematic than *ministry*. This is not because it's a bad word in itself, but mainly because of the way it is unwittingly used to support a secular/spiritual split. It often has the effect of elevating certain types of service above others, making them appear more "spiritual" or important.

"My ministry is encouraging people." "I'm in the ministry." "We held a time of ministry at the end of the service." "ABC Ministries seeks to . . ." "Let me minister to you." The words *ministry* and *minister* are used in countless different ways, usually in some sense to highlight the "spiritual" nature of the task or role. But what does the word really mean? Paul Stevens comments:

> The word *ministry* is derived in both Greek and Hebrew from a word that simply means "service." A Christian servant is someone who puts himself or herself at God's disposal for the benefit of others and for the stewardship of God's world. Christian service—commonly called ministry—accords with God's purposes for people and the world and has the touch of God, often unknown to the servant. Christian service makes no distinction between the sacred and the secular. Washing dishes, designing a computer program, preaching a sermon and healing the sick are all one.[1]

Given the way this word is so badly abused, we may do better to replace *ministry* with *Christian service* or just *service*. Not only will this help to work against our dualism, but it will also have the effect of putting all service (given to God) on an even footing.

CALLING AND VOCATION

Calling is one word that is worth "redeeming," if only because there is no easy alternative. *Vocation* would have been the obvious candidate, but over the last few centuries it has been thoroughly "secularized" and watered down to mean something far less than originally intended. We suggest, however, that you aim to use the word *calling* with some discrimination. Be careful and selective in its use (chapter 8, "Work as Calling," helps to fill out the biblical meaning of the term). Used in the right sense and context, it can be a powerful word, connecting who we are and what we do with our source and leader, Jesus.

"WHAT DO YOU DO?"

Perhaps the most defining question in our culture is the introductory question, "What do you do?" It says a lot in itself. Notice it doesn't say, "Who are you?" or "What's important to you?" Of course, we must be careful not to read too much into this culturally polite small talk. In itself it's a good way of inviting people to share about themselves. As we've seen, however, the problem is what it implies: the suggestion that who we are and what we're worth as people is wrapped up in our occupation. As if your paid employment could define your identity as a person! (Worse, what it says about people who aren't paid for the work they do is depressing. Does this make them less than full persons?)

It's worth pointing out that our own culture's introductory question is not always as innocent as it may appear. Often it contributes to the status games our society encourages us to play. Tony Campolo tells of how his wife Peggy grew tired of the points-scoring at dinner and cocktail parties, and the way it made her feel so worthless. For example, she would ask a young woman what she did for a job, and the woman would reply something like, "I'm a lawyer with Bond, Gibbon, and Priest, specializing in commercial law and public policy. And what do you do?" Flattened, Peggy would usually offer apologetically, "Oh, I'm just a housewife."

Determined no longer to be intimidated, she worked out a patter (a planned response). At the next dinner party, when asked what she did, Peggy replied seriously, "I'm involved in the socialization of two Homo sapiens into the dominant values of the Judeo-Christian tradition so that they might be transformers of the social order into the kind of eschatological utopia God willed for us before the foundation of the world," or words to that effect. The incident is a salutary insight into the power of grand phrases, for when as an apparent afterthought Peggy asked, "And what do you do?" her unnerved acquaintance could only manage, "Oh, I'm just a lawyer"!

Perhaps those of us with less definable working weeks or with low status occupations could design a reply patter like Peggy! But just as important is thinking about what we can do to disengage some of the "power" that goes with this small question. What about using some alternatives such as, "What does your week consist of?" or "Tell me a little about yourself."

A CAUTION

In offering the suggestions in this chapter, we are conscious that we are at risk of stepping into another trap that has beset Christians over the centuries—the trap of laying down yet another set of rules. Nothing could be worse than creating a group of buzzwords that mark out our so-called spiritual maturity. So let us emphasize that these are just suggestions, ways to break the pattern of thinking that has bedeviled the church from its earliest days. For words *do* matter. They often give subtle messages about how we value people, indicating how we think about what others spend their lives doing. So, without setting up a new legalism, let's take a little trouble to use words carefully and help them carry the meaning we intend.

⁞⁞⁞⁞⁞⁞⁞⁞⁞⁞⁞⁞⁞⁞⁞⁞⁞⁞⁞⁞⁞⁞⁞⁞⁞⁞⁞⁞⁞⁞⁞⁞⁞⁞⁞⁞⁞⁞UP CLOSE & PERSONAL

1. Can you think of other words or phrases that are problematic in working against a biblical view of work? Suggest some good alternatives.

2. Within the life of your own faith community, what are some of the assumptions that deserve to be challenged? Are there words and terminology that should be more transparent, honest, or unambiguous?

EXERCISE

Refer back to the list of roles and tasks you made at the end of the introduction. Try to group them into the four spheres of involvement: marketplace, family, community, and church. Remembering that these spheres can overlap, which sphere dominates your time and energy?

14

REAL WORK FOR REAL PEOPLE

The Ongoing Journey

Remember our characters from the beginning of the book? Let's look at them now after the course of this study to discover the various issues raised for them along the way. Let's see how they are doing on this journey of connecting their work with God's work.

ROGER

Perspectives That Have Been Helpful

Roger, with his academically trained mind, had no difficulty understanding the theological meaning of the word *vocation*. He easily coped with the idea that he was not called to be a lawyer but to follow Christ—and that one outworking of that call was serving Jesus through his profession.

From there it wasn't a big step for Roger to see that his role as a parent was not just an add-on. In fact, this insight was freeing to him, because he had nursed guilty feelings about his "absent father" workaholism. Theologically and theoretically, he jumped at the chance to value parenthood, to see it as central to his efforts at this stage of his life—that is, a wonderful opportunity for discipleship.

Habits That Are Changing

Roger has even managed to translate a little of this into action. He sets himself the task of getting home regularly for the evening meal (though he fails as much as he succeeds in this goal!), and he has deliberately scheduled into his diary a slot on Saturdays for accompanying his children to their sport. Again, it doesn't always work out, but he has made some effort.

Unresolved Issues

Roger, however, still has a long way to go. The problem is his drivenness. Secretly, he genuinely believes he is indispensable. He doesn't yet have a big enough view of God's sovereignty. He still has to learn that this is God's work and that he is a junior partner.

Unanswered Questions

Until he recognizes his egocentric thinking, Roger will still struggle with the questions that bother him, which he frequently expresses to his wife Colleen: How do I keep all the balls in the air? I feel like it's a perpetual juggling act. How can I put some limits on the time and energy I need to give to my paid employment? Where can I get the energy to spend time with the kids at night? By the time I get home, I just want to crash in front of the screen. How can I politely get out of some of the church jobs I've accumulated? How do I learn to say no?

More important questions he still has to grapple with are: How do I learn to rest biblically? How do I recognize that God's work is best served if I see that my role is more in relating with people (including my children), and less in the tasks I undertake?

Possible Directions for Roger to Pursue

Roger could profitably undertake some sessions with a counselor who could help him identify and deal with his compulsion for seeking affirmation and approval—which is probably rooted in a childhood need to perform for one or more of the adults in his life. When he recognizes this problem, he can then devise strategies for dealing with it, and he will finally discover the freedom to say no.

KAREN

Habits That Are Changing

Karen has worked through the issues in this book with a small study group to which she and her husband Steve belong. Encouraged by the others in the group, she is determined to tackle head-on the people who leave her feeling put down because of her full-time role as a mother. She has borrowed Peggy Campolo's idea and has worked out several replies to the "What do you do?" question.

Perspectives That Have Been Helpful

The idea of partnering with God has begun to radically alter the way Karen thinks about her daily tasks. She feels motivated to take even more seriously the challenge of raising her sons, relating to her unchurched friends, and helping out at school. Karen has also been inspired to see that if God himself has taken on mundane, maintenance tasks, then even the dirty washing and the constant cleaning up after the family is of value.

Unresolved Issues

Karen faces the problem of many full-time mothers—feeling isolated and trapped in an unstimulating environment. She yearns for the intellectual and social growth that her husband Steve enjoys as a teacher.

Unanswered Questions

What happens when my children grow up? What can I do long term in God's service? Should I think about training myself for a future career? I enjoy the children and helping people through my church contacts, but does that sort of practical assistance help me for the next stage of my life? Am I allowing myself to be sidelined?

Possible Directions for Karen to Pursue

Karen might usefully engage in part-time training to enhance her people-caring skills. This training might be in health areas (such as nursing) or educational or practical ones, depending on where her interests take her. She might, for example, consider equipping herself to eventually become a teacher, a counselor, an aid worker, a staff member in a service organization, or an advocate for disadvantaged people.

JOSEPH

Perspectives That Have Been Helpful

Joseph has caught on to the idea that work is much bigger and broader than "paid employment," but unfortunately that's as far as he has travelled. This inadequate understanding has just reinforced for him that his job at the bank should be treated as a means to an end.

Habits That Are Changing

For Joseph nothing has changed. A certain glamour is still attached in his mind to the idea of "full-time Christian service." He can't help thinking that if he were to find some such position, it would give an immediate lift to his spiritual maturity. Then at last he wouldn't feel so ineffectual in his life for God. Until Joseph's understanding of what God is about in this world begins to change, there likely won't be any deepening of his contribution to the world of his employment.

Unresolved Issues

Joseph still can't get his mind around the false division between secular and spiritual, and the resulting value judgments over what tasks are particularly important to God. That sort of thinking is just too deeply embedded in his psyche, so he continues to struggle with the apparent futility of his banking job. He hasn't yet been able to explore the range of opportunities that his employment offers—the ways he could make a difference here and now.

Unanswered Questions

For Joseph, these relate mainly to issues of guidance. What do I do with this strong "call" I feel I have to "the ministry"? And if I don't pursue that leading, then won't it mean disaster for the rest of my life because I will have missed God's perfect will for me?

Possible Directions for Joseph to Pursue

If Joseph's friends could steer him into some such service opportunity as hospital chaplaincy, industrial chaplaincy, or as a counselor on a crisis phone line (like Samaritans or Lifeline)—a short term of "volunteer service" might do the trick—he could be brought to see what huge contributions Christians can make alongside ordinary people.

MARK

Perspectives That Have Been Helpful

Mark has wrestled with his difficulties as an overworked middle manager and is beginning to get a handle on his problem. His thinking has gone like this: God has me working in the company for a real purpose—not just for earning money and the occasional sharing of my faith with others. So much for step one. Mark has caught on to the concept of working with God to be an agent of change.

Habits That Are Changing

Step two. He's made an agreement with his wife that he won't bring work home during the weekends. Having drawn this line in the sand, Mark has been able to come to terms with the risk of losing his job. He's decided that there's more to his life than his well-paid employment.

Step three. He has therefore taken the step of talking (cautiously) with his manager about acceptable limits to his workload—and found the manager surprisingly receptive. Between them they've agreed that 50 hours of full-on effort is reasonable.

Unresolved Issues

The emotional stress of the above three steps occupied Mark for some time. He's only now finding himself ready to look at the next question. While he sees clearly how unredeemed his employment environment is, he hasn't yet worked out how he can make a difference in the atmosphere of mistrust, low morale, and straight-out dishonesty that exists in the company. Significantly, he also hasn't been able to find other Christians who will help him work through appropriate responses to the myriad issues he is becoming aware of.

Unanswered Questions

For Mark, there is still no clear connection between Sunday and the rest of the week. He finds the worship service frustratingly irrelevant.

Possible Directions for Mark to Pursue

Mark can profit enormously from finding like-minded friends among his Christian acquaintances. Joining a study group that wants to investigate these issues would be a huge help.

JULIE

Perspectives That Have Been Helpful

For Julie, thinking biblically about work and God's call has been a breakthrough. "Unemployed at 58" has given way to "a future of service for God wherever he takes me." She doesn't just see the potential of what God wants to do in the world—she sees potential in her own abilities and experience for being part of God's work!

Habits That Are Changing

With impressive speed, she has abandoned her past mood of procrastination and inadequacy. She has looked at herself in the mirror (literally, because that's how she made the determination to change) and said: "Julie Irvine, God has so much that you could be doing with him. You don't have time to sit around and mope. For the next month, watch what crosses your path and see how you can get involved as God's agent of change!"

Unresolved Issues

For the most part, these are just determining how to discriminate between all the things she sees that *could* be done and the practical sense of how much she *can* take on. ("Julie Irvine," she said to her mirror just the other day, "Don't be an idiot. You may be a child of God with a brilliant eternal destiny, but you *are* 58. You're not going to be able to sort out the whole world this year. Now sit down carefully before you go promising your support to every organization under the sun. You have to make priorities. Which one—or maybe two—will you commit yourself to?")

Unanswered Questions

"Julie Irvine, how long have you got? Better add an exercise program to your daily schedule!"

Possible Directions for Julie to Pursue

As you can see, Julie's new sense of freedom has released a bubbly enthusiasm! There's not much to add to Julie's good sense, except to suggest that she might find others in the same situation. She could be a marvelous model for them and could help them find a whole new realm of service for God.

REFLECTION

What about you? Now is a good time to reflect on what you've absorbed during the course of reading this book. Why not take some time to think about:

- Some perspectives that have been helpful
- Some habits that are changing
- Some unresolved issues
- Some unanswered questions
- Some directions you might pursue

A PRAYER FOR OUR WORK

Dear Lord,

We thank you that you are a worker, and you invite us to share in your work as your partners. We confess that sometimes we work in ways that ignore what you are doing, pretending we don't need you or that we can make a difference without you. Forgive us for when we work compulsively, as though what we're doing is the most important thing on earth. Forgive us when we treat our work as little more than a means to an end. Forgive us when we fail to see that all work done in cooperation with you is good and worthwhile.

As we enter a new week of work, we acknowledge afresh our dependence on you in all we put our hands to. Help us to find dignity and purpose in every task—particularly, Lord, in what we find mundane or hard. Give us vision to see where you are already working—in our homes and families, in our neighborhoods, in our places of employment, in our church life, and in our surroundings. Fuel us with imagination to see what you want us to do. Give us humility to serve without complaint, in whatever tasks are before us. Transform us as we work. Help us make this week of work an act of worship.

May your kingdom come here on earth (particularly in our places of work) just as it is in heaven. We ask this all in the name of the One who modeled what it is to work with and for you.

Amen.

EPILOGUE

Why We Wrote This Book

ALISTAIR'S STORY

As Calvin Redekop has noted (whom we mentioned in chapter 1), the truth is that average Christians spend less than 2 percent of their waking time at church and most of their time working. Yet the church puts most of its energy and resources into that 2 percent and very little into the world of daily work.

When I first read Redekop's words many years ago, they haunted me and as a pastor I felt challenged. The church's largest mission force mobilizes in the world every day of the week when Christians go about their daily work, but I was doing little to intentionally resource and support people for this missionary encounter. In fact, I was not sure that most of my congregation even realized the importance of their daily work.

SURVEY

As a result of my disquiet, I began doing a lot of reading on the subject. It occurred to me, however, that nothing could compare with actually talking to Christians face-to-face about how they understood the connection of their faith with their work. As a result, I spent six months conducting one hundred in-depth interviews with individuals from predominantly evangelical, charismatic, and Pentecostal church backgrounds, along with a number of discussion groups, seminars, and informal encounters. The results of this survey changed my understanding—and my life! Here's what I discovered.

Work Is for Evangelism and Money

Most people interviewed assumed that I wanted to talk with them about how they were doing in evangelizing their workmates, and the majority said (in a way that made both of us feel uncomfortable) that they weren't very good at it. The fact that this was their immediate assumption betrayed their significant discomfort with what they thought about evangelism. It also became obvious that the majority of these interviewees assumed their church valued their employment only for the purposes of evangelism and earning money to support the church and parachurch ministries.

Two Distinct Groups

At the same time, there did appear to be two distinct groups when it came to how people felt God viewed their work. On the one hand, there were those in what we might label the "helping professions"—doctors, nurses, social workers, teachers, counselors, and so on. These people were generally happy to use the word *ministry* regarding their work in some sense. They generally saw ways their "people-helping" work counted from God's perspective and felt the church affirmed the worth of these roles.

The other group, however, consisted of people involved as factory workers, manufacturers, businesspersons, office workers, computer programmers, engineers, and other commercial or industrial workers. These people seldom talked about their work as a form of ministry, unless it concerned talking to people about their faith. They struggled to find specific ways to connect their work to their faith, particularly if their work had little to do with helping people.

Hierarchy of Value

Underlying many of these comments was a powerful hierarchy of value. While there was a general acceptance that all Christians were equal, clearly some were more equal than others. Those assumed to be of most value to God (and the church) were missionaries and pastors, followed by other "full-time Christian workers," and then elders and deacons. Then there were those involved as volunteers in church activities. At the bottom of the pile were those Christians solely involved in full-time "secular" work. Although many interviewees didn't think it should be like this, most thought that in practice this was how it was.

Absence of Connection between Church and Work

Glaringly obvious in these interviews was the inability of people to recall any significant connecting points between their church experience and their work. In particular:

- Most people could not remember ever hearing a *sermon* or teaching on work.

- Only a couple of people could identify any *songs* sung in church that referred to work.

- Few were able to recall any *prayers* prayed specifically about work, with the exception of ones referring to evangelism. (There were a few Episcopalians and Catholics who thought there might have been some reference to work in the intercessory portion of their liturgies, though they couldn't remember the details.)

- Only rarely did work come up as a topic in church *small group discussions* or studies, although most pastors felt this was where people actually talked about their work.

- People's perception was that their *church leaders were not interested* in their work. Most had never been visited by a church leader at work. Additionally, most businesspeople felt their church leaders had a predominantly negative view of business, because they used only negative examples of business ethics in their preaching.

- Hardly any person was able to think of a particular Christian role model engaged in the marketplace (apart from sports stars, pop stars, or one or two politicians—mainly William Wilberforce).

- Most had never read a *book* or attended any *course* that talked about faith and work issues.

- Most people felt that church was competing with work and family in a way they didn't feel good about. This left me with the feeling that faith had become associated with another set of time commitments, rather than part of the essential glue helping people integrate complex and pressured lives.

- Increasingly, people were experiencing more ethical dilemmas in a more pluralistic marketplace.

- Many interviewees said they would also appreciate help with career and life-planning decisions.

The Problem of Other Christians at Work

Then there was the issue we noted in chapter 9, "Work as Worship." In answer to the question, "What is the most difficult thing you experience as a Christian at work?" many interviewees replied, "The other Christians I work with." When I inquired why, their reasons ranged from the embarrassment of super-spiritual workmates who were excessively zealous in their talk about their faith and attempts to evangelize, but who were not so serious about their work, to the sub-Christian behavior of those who publicly identified themselves as believers. This negative feedback didn't just relate to employees, either. The poor ethics of some "Christian" firms and employers was cited as a major source of embarrassment in some industries. The major issue was not whether people identified themselves as Christians, but what kind of Christians they were.

CONCLUSIONS

The overwhelming impression I gained was that most Christians felt resigned to the fact that church life did not really relate to what they spent much of their week involved in. The majority weren't motivated enough to do something about this without assistance. Neither did they feel that church leaders understood the kinds of work pressures and demands they experienced.

Of course, people would have loved it to be different. In fact, there was a real yearning for encouragement and help, and the longer I chatted with many, the more animated they became as they realized I was serious about exploring the wider implications of faith for their work. I concluded that in order for Christians to gain and nurture an ongoing sense of vocation (or "SoulPurpose," as I came to call it), there were five important ingredients.

1. *Connection.* Understanding that our work and God's work are connected. Gaining a sense that we are participating in something of ultimate significance, that imparts purpose to our lives. Involving both a biblical view that affirms the worth of our work (theology) and discovering ways we can nurture a sense of the presence of God in our work (spirituality).

2. *Fit*. Feeling that each of us fits the work we are doing. This is partly about understanding how our gifted-ness (abilities, talents, passions, personality) makes us unique and should help to define the kind of work we are best fitted for. But it also involves an ethical fit, so that we not only work well but also believe in the worth of what we are doing, and that we are able to see how it fits with our Christian calling and values.

3. *Service*. Christians are not happy in the long term serving only themselves. We need to be able to see how our work is making a worthwhile investment in God's wider purposes and in the lives of other people. We want to help create a better world.

4. *Balance*. Establishing a healthy balance in our lives that enables us to express our vocation through a mix of unpaid domestic and voluntary work, rest and leisure, and paid employment. Finding a sense of meaning and integration in the whole of our lives, and being able to renegotiate this balance at different stages of life.

5. *Encouragement*. Having the support and encourage-ment of a community of committed companions, which might include family, friends, and mentors, but which also needs to include our faith community.

HELPFUL RESOURCES

While it's been nearly twenty years since I conducted this survey, I can still recall many of the conversations. They have helped set the course for much of what I have put my hand to since. This book is one of the outcomes, along with two other books Wayne and I have written together: *SoulPurpose: Mak-*

ing a Difference in Life and Work and *Just Decisions: Christian Ethics Go to Work*. Additionally, you may like to visit our websites: www.faithatwork.org.nz (Alistair's), and www.ruminations .co.nz (Wayne's).

There is also a biblical commentary on what the Bible says about work, along with corresponding Bible studies, produced by the Theology of Work Project and published by Hendrickson Publishers (www.hendrickson.com). For more information on the Theology of Work Project, including an online version of the commentary with sidebar articles and videos, visit www .theologyofwork.org.

BIBLIOGRAPHY

Banks, Robert. *God the Worker: Journeys into the Mind, Heart, and Imagination of God.* Sutherland, NSW: Albatross, 1992. Reprint, Eugene, OR: Wipf & Stock, 2008.

Brinn, Steve. Quoted in R. Paul Stevens, *Doing God's Business: Meaning and Motivation for the Marketplace.* Grand Rapids: Eerdmans, 2006.

Brother Lawrence. *The Practice of the Presence of God: With Spiritual Maxims.* Grand Rapids: Revell, 1999.

Diehl, William E. *Christianity and Real Life.* Philadelphia: Fortress, 1976.

Evans, Craig. *Luke.* New International Bible Commentary. Peabody, MA: Hendrickson, 1990.

Fee, Gordon. *1 Corinthians.* New International Commentary on the New Testament. Grand Rapids: Eerdmans, 1987.

Foster, Richard J. "A Prayer at Mid-day." *Prayers from the Heart.* New York: HarperCollins, 1994.

Guinness, Os. "The Recovery of Vocation for Our Time" (unpublished audiotape). Quoted in R. Paul Stevens, *The Other Six Days: Vocation, Work, and Ministry in Biblical Perspective.* Grand Rapids: Eerdmans, 2000.

Lencioni, Patrick. *The Three Signs of a Miserable Job: A Fable for Managers (And Their Employees).* San Francisco: Jossey-Bass, 2007.

MacDonald, Gordon. "Rest Stops." *Life@Work Journal* 2, no. 4.

Mackenzie, Alistair, and Wayne Kirkland. *Just Decisions: Christian Ethics Go to Work*. Christchurch, NZ: NavPress, 2008.

―――. *SoulPurpose: Making a Difference in Life and Work*. Christchurch, NZ: NavPress, 2004.

Marshall, Paul. "Callings: Spirituality, Work and Duty in Sixteenth and Seventeenth-Century England." Unpublished manuscript, 1993.

―――. "Work." *New Dictionary of Christian Ethics and Pastoral Theology*. Edited by David J. Atkinson, David F. Field, Arthur F. Holmes, and Oliver O'Donovan. Downers Grove, IL: IVP Academic, 1995.

Motyer, J. Alec. *The Prophecy of Isaiah: An Introduction and Commentary*. Downers Grove, IL: InterVarsity Press, 1993.

Peterson, Eugene. *A Long Obedience in the Same Direction: Discipleship in an Instant Society*. Downers Grove, IL: IVP Books, 1980.

Ringma, Charles. "Theology of the Laity." Quoted in R. Paul Stevens, *The Other Six Days: Vocation, Work, and Ministry in Biblical Perspective*. Grand Rapids: Eerdmans, 2000.

Stevens, R. Paul. "Calling/Vocation" and "Ministry." *The Complete Book of Everyday Christianity*. Edited by Robert Banks and R. Paul Stevens. Downers Grove, IL: IVP, 1997.

Stott, John R. W. *Issues Facing Christians Today*. Basingstoke, UK: Marshalls, 1984. Reprint, Grand Rapids: Zondervan, 2006.

Theology of Work Project. *Theology of Work Bible Commentary*. 5 vols. Peabody, MA: Hendrickson, 2014–2015.

Walsh, Brian J., and J. Richard Middleton. *The Transforming Vision: Shaping a Christian World View*. Grand Rapids: IVP Academic, 1984.

Wright, N. T. *Colossians and Philemon*. Tyndale New Testament Commentaries. Downers Grove, IL: IVP Academic, 1986.

Wuthnow, Robert. *God and Mammon in America*. New York: Free Press, 1998.

NOTES

INTRODUCTION

1. Paul Marshall, "Work," in *New Dictionary of Christian Ethics and Pastoral Theology*, ed. David J. Atkinson, David F. Field, Arthur F. Holmes, and Oliver O'Donovan (Downers Grove, IL: IVP Academic, 1995), 899.

2. John R. Stott, *Issues Facing Christians Today* (Basingstoke, UK: Marshalls, 1984; repr., Grand Rapids: Zondervan, 2006), 162.

CHAPTER 1

1. Eugene Peterson, *A Long Obedience in the Same Direction: Discipleship in an Instant Society* (Downers Grove, IL: IVP Books, 1980), 104.

2. Robert Banks, *God the Worker: Journeys into the Mind, Heart, and Imagination of God* (Sutherland, NSW: Albatross, 1992; repr., Eugene, OR: Wipf & Stock, 2008).

CHAPTER 4

1. J. Alec Motyer, *The Prophecy of Isaiah: An Introduction and Commentary* (Downers Grove, IL: InterVarsity Press, 1993), 321.

CHAPTER 5

1. Craig Evans, *Luke*, New International Bible Commentary (Peabody, MA: Hendrickson, 1990), 196.

CHAPTER 6

1. Gordon MacDonald, "Rest Stops," in *Life@Work Journal* 2, no. 4.

CHAPTER 7

1. N. T. Wright, *Colossians and Philemon*, Tyndale New Testament Commentaries (Downers Grove, IL: IVP Academic, 1986), 149–50.

2. Eugene Peterson, *A Long Obedience in the Same Direction: Discipleship in an Instant Society (Downers Grove, IL: IVP Books,* 1980), 70.

3. R. Paul Stevens, "Calling/Vocation," in *The Complete Book of Everyday Christianity*, ed. Robert Banks and R. Paul Stevens (Downers Grove, IL: IVP, 1997), 97–102.

4. Paul Marshall, "Callings: Spirituality, Work and Duty in Sixteenth and Seventeenth-Century England" (unpublished manuscript, 1993).

5. Richard J. Foster, "A Prayer at Mid-day," in *Prayers from the Heart* (New York: HarperCollins, 1994), 76.

CHAPTER 8

1. Os Guinness, "The Recovery of Vocation for Our Time" (unpublished audiotape), quoted in R. Paul Stevens, *The Other Six Days: Vocation, Work, and Ministry in Biblical Perspective* (Grand Rapids: Eerdmans, 2000), 77.

2. Gordon Fee, *1 Corinthians*, New International Commentary on the New Testament (Grand Rapids: Eerdmans, 1987), 307.

CHAPTER 9

1. Brother Lawrence, *The Practice of the Presence of God: With Spiritual Maxims* (Grand Rapids: Revell, 1999), 115.

2. Brother Lawrence, 98.

CHAPTER 10

1. William E. Diehl, *Christianity and Real Life* (Philadelphia: Fortress, 1976), v–vi.

2. Charles Ringma, "Theology of the Laity," quoted in R. Paul Stevens, *The Other Six Days: Vocation, Work, and Ministry in Biblical Perspective* (Grand Rapids: Eerdmans, 2000), 203–4.

3. Eugene Peterson, *A Long Obedience in the Same Direction: Discipleship in an Instant Society* (Downers Grove, IL: IVP Books, 1980), 106–7.

4. Brian J. Walsh and J. Richard Middleton, *The Transforming Vision: Shaping a Christian World View* (Grand Rapids: IVP Academic, 1984).

5. Steve Brinn, quoted in R. Paul Stevens, *Doing God's Business: Meaning and Motivation for the Marketplace* (Grand Rapids: Eerdmans, 2006), 98.

CHAPTER 11

1. See Patrick Lencioni, *The Three Signs of a Miserable Job: A Fable for Managers (And Their Employees)* (San Francisco: Jossey-Bass, 2007).

CHAPTER 12

1. Disturbingly, sociologist Robert Wuthnow discovered that for many people with religious faith, ethics in the workplace is essentially viewed as the need to be "honest," and that even this word is thought of in quite narrow terms. As Wuthnow argues, with this truncated perspective "one's behaviour may contribute to the burning of rain forests and the perpetuation of world hunger and yet, as long as one tells the truth, ethics is not a problem." Robert Wuthnow, *God and Mammon in America* (New York: Free Press, 1998), 84.

2. This is not to suggest that there won't be some points of commonality to the way other car dealerships were run.

CHAPTER 13

1. R. Paul Stevens, "Ministry," in *The Complete Book of Everyday Christianity*, ed. Robert Banks and R. Paul Stevens (Downers Grove, IL: IVP, 1997), 635.

About the Hendrickson Publishers/ Theology of Work Line of Books

There is an unprecedented interest today in the role of Christian faith in "ordinary" work, and Christians in every field are exploring what it means to work "as to the Lord" (Col. 3:22). Pastors and church leaders, and the scholars and teachers who support them, are asking what churches can do to equip their members in the workplace. There's a need for deep thinking, fresh perspectives, practical ideas, and mutual engagement between Christian faith and work in every sphere of human endeavor.

This Hendrickson Publishers/Theology of Work line of books seeks to bring significant new resources into this conversation. It began with Hendrickson's publication of the *Theology of Work Bible Commentary* and other Bible study materials written by the TOW Project. Soon we discovered a wealth of resources by other writers with a common heart for the meaning and value of everyday work. The HP/TOW line was formed to make the best of these resources available on the national and international stage.

Works in the HP/TOW line engage the practical issues of daily work through the lens of the Bible and the other resources of the Christian faith. They are biblically grounded, but their subjects are the work, workers, and workplaces of today. They employ contemporary arts and sciences, best practices, empirical research, and wisdom gained from experience, yet always in the service of Christ's redemptive work in the world, especially the world of work.

To a greater or lesser degree, all the books in this line make use of the scholarship of the *Theology of Work Bible Commentary*. The authors, however, are not limited to the TOW Project's perspectives, and they constantly expand the scope and application of the material. Publication of a book in the HP/TOW line does not necessarily imply endorsement by the Theology of Work Project, or that the author endorses the TOW Project. It does mean we recognize the work as an important contribution to the faith-work discussion, and we find a common footing that makes us glad to walk side-by-side in the dialogue.

We are proud to present the HP/TOW line together. We hope it helps readers expand their thinking, explore ideas worthy of deeper thought, and make sense of their own work in light of the Christian faith. We are grateful to the authors and all those whose labor has brought the HP/TOW line to life.

William Messenger, Executive Editor, Theology of Work Project
Sean McDonough, Biblical Editor, Theology of Work Project
Patricia Anders, Editorial Director, Hendrickson Publishers

www.theologyofwork.org
www.hendrickson.com

"This commentary was written exactly for those of
us who aim to integrate our faith and work on a
daily basis and is an excellent reminder that God
hasn't called the world to go to the church,
but has called the Church to go to the world."

BONNIE WURZBACHER
FORMER SENIOR VICE PRESIDENT, THE COCA-COLA COMPANY